Ajanta

Ajanta

Regional Feasts of India

LACHU MOORJANI

PHOTOGRAPHY BY MARTY SNORTUM

Gibbs Smith, Publisher
Salt Lake City

First Edition
09 08 07 06 05   5 4 3 2 1

Text © 2005 by Lachu Moorjani
Photographs © 2005 by Marty Snortum
Food styling by Harriett Granthen

Published by
Gibbs Smith, Publisher
P.O. Box 667
Layton, Utah 84041

Orders: 1.800.748.5439
www.gibbs-smith.com

Designed by Ron Stucki
Printed and bound in Hong Kong

Library of Congress Cataloging-in-Publication Data

Moorjani, Lachu.
   Ajanta : regional feasts of India / Lachu Moorjani ;
Photographs by Marty Snortum.
      p. cm.
   ISBN 1-58685-777-0
   1. Cookery, India. 2. Ajanta (Restaurant) I. Ajanta
(Restaurant) II. Title.

TX724.5.I4M663 2005
641.5954—dc22

                        2005012295

Contents

Bharwan Mirch Pakora (Stuffed Chile Pepper Fritters)

Kheeray Ka Raita (Yogurt Cucumber Raita)

Rasgulla (Paneer Cheese Balls in Syrup)

Acknowledgments

I WOULD LIKE TO THANKFULLY ACKNOWLEDGE the inspiration and help given to me by:

My mother and my sisters. While growing up, had it not been for their great cooking, I am not sure I would have learned how to appreciate and enjoy good food.

Countless number of my restaurant customers who suggested to me that I should write a cookbook.

My students and my friends who participated in my cooking classes and cooking parties. Aside from testing the recipes, I learned as much from them as they did from me.

My wife, Shanti, who helped me perfect my recipes through cooking classes and cooking parties in our home kitchen.

My friend Janice Flatto for correcting my grammar and editing my writing.

Gibbs Smith and his editorial staff, for bringing this book to a reality.

Naan Bread (Flat Bread Made with Leavened Dough) in Tandoor Oven

Introduction

FOOD HAS ALWAYS BEEN A PASSION FOR ME. I grew up in a small town in northern India. We did not have a refrigerator, so buying fresh vegetables and meat every day and eating freshly cooked meals was a way of life for us. My mother was an excellent cook and my whole family craved and enjoyed good food. Even today, I vividly recall how some of these home-cooked dishes tasted when I was going to grade school in Bikaner, Rajasthan.

I was born in the state of Sindh, India, in 1941. Sindh became Pakistan in 1947, and at that time my parents moved to Rajasthan, where I grew up. I studied engineering there and graduated in 1962. I then moved to Bombay to work as an industrial engineer. One of the early projects I worked on was to introduce standard cost and budgetary controls in a factory, in the cafeteria and the officer's club. About two thousand meals were prepared and served every day in these facilities. The project required me to weigh each of the ingredients the cooks used for all the dishes they prepared, in order to set the standards for the material cost. I also did time studies to set the labor costs. These studies required me to stand and watch everything the cooks did in preparing the dishes. I loved this project. I got an in-depth exposure to food preparation and cooking techniques, and felt I learned more about cooking doing this engineering project than I could have almost anywhere else. This inspired me to do some cooking at home and to create dishes that were not in my family repertoire.

The food I prepared at home up to this time was generally Sindhi dishes, Rajasthani dishes, and North Indian dishes. The engineering project at the factory cafeteria had also introduced me to South Indian cooking, as that was the background of most of the cooks working there. Around that time, one of my sisters married a man from Goa. My new brother-in-law and his family introduced me to Goanese cooking. In the homes of my friends in Bombay, I tasted Maharashtra and Parsee cooking. During five years of living in Bombay, I came to know and appreciate the differences in flavors of food from various regions of India.

In December of 1969, I immigrated to the United States and lived on my own in Berkeley, California. At this time, the search for good food became very important for me. The first book I bought in the United States was *The Underground Gourmet* by R. B. Read. I also searched out the restaurant reviews published in the *Chronicle* and other newspapers and magazines. Armed with this information, I systematically started to visit the best restaurants in the Bay Area and eat the best food I could afford. Very soon, I developed a reputation among my friends for being a walking encyclopedia of good restaurants in the Bay Area, and they often consulted me before going out to eat.

My dining experience in Indian restaurants in the San Francisco Bay Area left me dissatisfied, however. I enjoyed the tandoori dishes, but the dishes cooked in sauces (or curries) always tasted stale and uninspired. I decided that to enjoy good Indian cooking, I would have to start cooking for myself in a serious way. So that is what I did. Soon my Indian friends began visiting my house for excellent Indian cuisine. By the early '70s, a couple of friends recruited me to open an Indian restaurant with them in San Francisco. I left my engineering job and cooked in the restaurant for a few months, but the partnership was short-lived and I went back to engineering. However, I made a decision to go back into the restaurant world when I could afford to open a restaurant of my own.

In December 1987, this opportunity came. I opened a small restaurant called New Delhi Junction in Berkeley. It offered good food at very reasonable prices, but it was in a poor location. Soon I realized that unless I did something different, the restaurant would fail. This was the beginning of a "changing menu," the first of its kind in any Indian restaurant in the Bay Area. I added a supplemental menu to the main menu, which featured three dishes from a region or state of India, and which changed every month. In this way, the diners had an opportunity to experience a wide variety of dishes from different regions of India. To further educate interested customers, I started to send out a newsletter in which I described the new dishes, along with a brief introduction to the region or the state where these dishes originated. During this time, I also increased my knowledge of Indian regional cooking substantially. I ate regional food whenever I visited India; read cookbooks; ate at friends' houses and asked them to share their recipes; and experimented at home before featuring dishes at the restaurant. And I enjoyed making changes to the recipes to make them more appealing to my palate.

With the success of New Delhi Junction, I felt the need to move to a larger location. In 1993, I sold New Delhi Junction and opened Ajanta. At Ajanta, I went a step further experimenting with recipes and the menu. Rather than having a supplemental menu with three dishes that changed monthly, the entire menu became subject to change. At Ajanta, three new dishes are added to the menu each month and three are discontinued. In this way, the entire menu changes in about four months. I also brought in new appetizers by introducing an "appetizer of the month." I continued to expand my repertoire of dishes and eventually I could go more than two years before repeating a dish. Eventually, in 2003, a small number of standard dishes were left on the menu to satisfy customer requests for these specific dishes.

About three years ago, I started to think about writing a cookbook and began to rework restaurant recipes for large crowds down to serving sizes for 6 to 8 people. I also started experimenting with new dishes and began conducting cooking classes at my home to refine the recipes. This cookbook is a collection of the best of the recipes I have produced in my many years in Indian restaurant cuisine. The book presents feasts from twelve different regions of India. Each dinner or feast includes an appetizer, main dish, side dish, rice dish, bread, and dessert. There are additional recipes for main and side dishes that can be substituted in these feasts for variety. Each chapter also includes a shopping list. Additional chapters give tips for Indian cooking and introduce ingredients that are specific to Indian cuisine.

It is my hope to introduce you to the best of Indian regional cooking through *Ajanta: Regional Feasts of India*. My recipes are authentic Indian cuisine, with a fusion of other elements to appeal to the western palate. The recipes are lighter than those in most other Indian cookbooks, and many original recipes include non-Indian ingredients, such as Portobello mushrooms and asparagus. Without any doubt, the recipes in this book are my best creations and the perfect dishes to bring you the fabulous feasts of regional Indian cuisine.

Tips for Good Indian Cooking

This chapter is essential reading for anyone interested in cooking good Indian food. You will get tips, advice, and helpful hints for ways of doing things that are not common in western cooking. You will also learn techniques unique to Indian cooking. Together this information will help you cook fabulous Indian fare.

Toasting Spices in Oil

Many recipes in this book require toasting spices in oil. Some seed spices (such as cumin, mustard, and fenugreek) are toasted in oil as a first step. For this to happen properly, it is very important that the oil is very hot. The oil should be almost, but not quite, smoking. This temperature will toast the seed spices without burning them. If the seed spices are added before the oil gets hot, it is likely that the spices will be burned rather than toasted.

Try this experiment at home. Put a couple of tablespoons of oil in a saucepan. Turn the heat on, and, without waiting for the oil to be hot, add a teaspoon of black mustard seeds. You will see that as the oil heats up, the seeds will slowly burn without popping. Now, repeat the same process, except this time wait until the oil is very hot before adding the seeds. When the seeds are added, they are toasted immediately and will pop and sputter in the pan.

An easy way to tell whether or not the oil is hot enough is to drop a couple of seeds in the oil. If the seeds sizzle and pop right away, then the oil is ready. If they do not, wait for a few seconds and try again.

Properly toasted spices give a wonderful aroma and flavor to the dishes in which they are used.

Using Whole Spices

Most Indian recipes call for spices in powdered form. Powdered spices lose their aroma and freshness when stored. Under ideal conditions, when sealed tightly and stored in a cool, dark place, powdered spices may last for 3 to 6 months. However, if you are cooking Indian food infrequently and storing your powdered spices, you will end up with spices that have become stale. Whole seed spices last much longer. I highly recommend buying spices whole and grinding them in small quantities as needed.

A coffee grinder works well for grinding spices. Some spices may be difficult to find whole (for example, dried turmeric); others are difficult to grind at home (for example, red chile peppers). For these spices, purchase them in powdered form in small quantities. Spices that can be purchased whole and ground as needed include coriander, cumin, cardamom, cinnamon, cloves, and fenugreek.

Kadhai for Frying

Traditional Indian cooking uses a specially formed, thick, wok-shaped pot for deep-frying called Kadhai. This pot allows a large surface for frying, while minimizing the oil used. Kadhai can be purchased in most Indian supply stores or you can find them online. Alternately, you can find a thick wok and use it for deep-frying (photo on page 224).

Frying Temperature

The correct frying temperature is essential to the success of a dish. For example, the well-known Indian dessert Gulab Jamun simply will not turn out right unless it is fried at a low temperature of about 300 degrees F. The temperature is also very important when frying appetizers such as Samosas and Pakoras. I recommend investing in a thermometer for measuring the temperature of hot oil.

Using Nonstick Pans

In Indian cooking, many recipes for main and side dishes require sautéing onions in oil. Onions have a tendency to stick to the bottom of the pot or pan during this process. You can keep the onions from sticking by stirring them very frequently, by turning down the heat (which increases cooking time), or by adding more oil. I recommend using nonstick pans to avoid the problem.

Flour for Indian Breads

Most Indian breads are made with whole wheat flour. Chapati Flour, available at local Indian grocery stores, is the best-suited flour for Indian breads. If there is no Indian grocer in your area, you can use finely ground (pastry grind), low-gluten whole wheat flour. Durum wheat is good low-gluten wheat, and pastry grind with Durum wheat flour should work well for Indian breads.

Basmati Rice

Literally translated, the word *Basmati* means "queen of fragrance." As its name suggests, Basmati is a variety of fragrant, long-grain rice that grows in North India and Pakistan. When cooked, this rice has a popcorn-like aroma and a nutty flavor. After eating Basmati rice a few times, you will find it hard to go back to regular rice. All the recipes in this cookbook specify the rice to be Basmati. This rice is currently so widely available that you can find it in regular grocery stores and even price clubs.

You should note that not all Basmati rice is good quality. It varies significantly in the quality as well as price. You can spend as little as 35 cents a pound and as much as a dollar or more a pound. High-quality Basmati rice is well worth the price, and I highly recommend using the best quality you can. In Indian grocery stores, price is generally a good indication of quality. Good Basmati rice will have thin, long grains. It has a distinctive aroma and the grains will separate when the rice is cooked.

Cooking Rice

Every good cook of Indian cuisine aspires to cook rice that does not stick together when it is fully cooked. Some cooks accomplish this by using less water—less than twice the amount of rice. This method, however, results in rice that is not completely cooked. Others recommend washing rice three or four times to get rid of the excess starch on the surface of rice. However, this method does not always result in properly cooked rice.

I have found a foolproof method for cooking rice that falls apart like pearls when it is cooked. Before cooking the rice, first sauté it in a small amount of oil. This seals in the starch. When the rice is cooked later on with water, it does not stick together and the kernels separate nicely.

Spiciness in the Recipes

One of the reasons some diners shy away from Indian food is their fear of hot spices. Many people, including some who love other spices, find it difficult to handle chile peppers. The recipes in this cookbook provide an easy solution to this problem. The quantity of chile pepper powder is usually shown in the recipe as "1/2 teaspoon to 2 teaspoons." Using 1/2 teaspoon in the recipe will give you a dish which is enjoyable in every respect without burning your taste buds. The more adventurous can use the full 2 teaspoons. Simply use as much chile pepper powder as your palate will permit.

Browning Meats

Most of the meat dishes in this book include a step for browning meats. Browning meat at high heat works better and results in a juicier meat, but when cooking for 6 or 8 people—unless you have a very high output burner on your range—this becomes difficult.

To brown meat at a high temperature, use your heaviest pot for cooking meats. Heat the pot at high heat for a while before adding meat. Heavy pots act as a heat sink and absorb heat, which is then transferred to the meat when it is added to the pot. Therefore, a heavy pot will brown the meat more efficiently. Whether or not you have a heavy pot, make sure that your meat is browned nicely and that the excess moisture is dried out before you proceed to the next step in the recipes.

Slicing or Chopping Onions

Indian cooking requires slicing or chopping a lot of onions. You can chop or slice onions in a specific way that makes this work easier. For recipes that call for slicing onions, first cut onions in two halves vertically, before peeling the onion. Then slice off about 1/4 inch from the top and bottom of each half. Then peel the onions; it is easier at this stage than peeling the whole onion. For dishes that call for thinly sliced onions, cut each half of the onion in 3 pieces vertically, and then thinly slice each piece in 1/16-inch

Peeling and slicing an onion

(or thinner) slices. Cut this way, onions become homogenized in the sauce when they are cooked.

For recipes that call for chopped onions, lay down half of the peeled onion on a cutting board on its flat side, make 1/8-inch vertical cuts, then slice the onion in 1/8-inch-thick slices.

Mixing Yogurt During Cooking

Many Indian recipes require adding yogurt to the sauces during cooking. Yogurt tends to curdle at high heat. Although this doesn't affect the final taste of the sauces, it mars the appearance and affects the presentation. To avoid curdling, turn down the heat on your sauce before adding the yogurt. Constantly stir the sauce while adding in the yogurt, then, once it is incorporated, turn the heat back up.

Cooking Time for Meat

Cooking times for meat in the recipes is general guidance only. The actual cooking time will vary and depends on several factors, including whether or not the meat is organic, the age of the animal, what the animal was fed, and so on. Always check to see if the meat is cooked through and has become tender before removing the dish from the stovetop or oven.

Have a Party!

I started testing my recipes in cooking classes. At first, these cooking classes were conducted in a local adult school. Later on, I taught from my home. Still later, rather than teaching classes, I started giving "cooking parties." At these parties, guests were given recipes, ingredients and utensils, and each person or team prepared one dish. Then we all shared the dishes and each other's labors! These parties were a lot of fun. Indian cooking is often labor intensive, and having cooking parties to prepare the regional feasts will make the cooking, as well as the eating, very enjoyable.

When cooking for yourself, don't feel compelled to cook the entire feast. It may be overwhelming to do so. Cooking just the rice and the main dish will definitely make an enjoyable meal.

Achari Baingan (Stuffed Eggplant)

Indian Ingredients and Spices

Indian cuisine probably uses more spices than any other cuisine in the world. It is not uncommon for Indian families to have 20 to 30 different spices in whole seeds or powder form. Armed with these spices, an Indian cook can produce dishes with more flavors than cooks from any other country can! Volatile oils in the spices, released during the process of cooking, appeal to the sense of smell and make the food very palatable. Sweet or pungent, aromatic and seductive, spices enhance the flavor of whatever dish they are added to.

This chapter provides a brief introduction to most spices and some additional ingredients used in Indian cooking. The ingredients are listed alphabetically. As you try different recipes in the book and become curious to know a little more about Indian spices and ingredients, you can refer to this chapter to help satisfy your curiosity.

If you happen to have an Indian grocery store in your area, it should have almost all the ingredients listed here. Many of these ingredients can also be found in large supermarkets. For hard-to-find spices, surfing the web should solve the problem.

Ajwain

A very pleasant tasting spice, Ajwain is similar to cumin/caraway seeds. It is generally used in seed form. Ajwain's flavor can be described as sharp, sweet and minty. The English name for this spice, bishop's weed, is not commonly known.

Asafetida
(Indian name – Hing)

Asafetida is a dried gum resin, obtained from Ferula, a species of plant related to fennel. Generally sold and used in powdered form, Asafetida is very intense in aroma and flavor and is therefore used in small quantities.

Bay Leaves
(Indian name – Tejpatta)

Leaves of *Laurus nobilis*, used generally in dried form, give a pleasant aroma to dishes. They are very commonly used in rice pilafs and biriyani dishes. In many parts of India, cassia leaves are used for the same purpose and also called tejpatta.

Black Cumin Seeds
(Indian name – Shahi Jeera)

Closely related to cumin, these seeds grow on the *Cuminum nigram* plant. They are used in North India in Kashmir and Moghlai cooking, almost always in seed form. The seeds are black in color; they are thinner than regular cumin seeds and milder in flavor.

Black Rock Salt
(Indian name – Kala Namak)

Mined from salt mines, this salt has a very distinctive, sulpher-like aroma and is almost always used in an Indian spice mixture called chaat masala. The black salt is not actually black, but reddish gray in rock form. It is generally used in ground form, which looks light purple in color.

Cardamom
(Indian name – Ilaichi)

A spice with a strong, sweetish flavor, cardamom is the fruit of the plant *Elletaria cardamomum*. The greenish pods have small black seeds. Cardamom is used whole, powdered or crushed in many desserts, rice dishes and curries. The spice mixture garam masala almost always includes cardamom. Cardamom usually refers to the small, green cardamom. Another variety of cardamom, black cardamom, is used frequently in rice pilaf to add an aromatic flavor.

Chickpea Flour
(Indian name – Besan)

Used to make batter for the very popular Indian snack Pakoras, chickpea flour is made by grinding dried, husked chickpeas. It is also used for thickening sauces (wheat flour is generally not used for this purpose in Indian cooking).

Chiles
(Indian name – Laal Mirch)

Almost all westerners, when asked about Indian food, respond by saying that Indian food is hot. Chile peppers, used in various ways, give it this characteristic. In Indian cuisine, chiles are used in all forms, including chopped green chiles, chile pepper powder, and crushed chiles. All provide heat in different ways to Indian dishes. Green chiles are immature pods of various peppers, ranging from mild to very hot depending on the type of peppers. One of the hottest varieties is habanero. Other very hot varieties are the cayenne, serrano and jalapeño. Most of the heat of the chile pepper is in the seeds and veins. These can be removed before cooking to reduce the amount of heat in the dish. Cooking for a long time also moderates the effect of chiles. Mature chiles turn red and are dried. These are sold in whole, crushed or powdered form and are used in dishes for different effects.

Always, always be very careful when handling chiles. After touching them, wash your hands very thoroughly with soap and water. Touching your eyes with unwashed hands after handling chiles will cause a very painful irritation.

Cinnamon
(Indian name – Dalchini)

Cinnamon is widely used in the United States and is a familiar spice to most cooks. It is the dried bark of the tree *Cinnamomum cassia*. Cinnamon harvested from a similar tree, *Cinnamomum zeylanicum*, is also sold as cinnamon, but does not have as strong a flavor as the one from cassia. Cinnamon is used in whole, quill form or in powder form to impart a sweet, aromatic flavor to desserts, rice and lentil dishes. Along with cardamom and cloves, cinnamon is a major component of the Indian spice mixture garam masala.

Cloves
(Indian name – Lavang)

The word *clove* is derived from the Latin *clavus* or the French *clou*, both meaning "nail," which describes the shape of this spice. Cloves are dried, unopened buds taken from the clove tree *Eugenia aromatica*. An aromatic, pungent spice with a strong flavor, cloves are generally used in small quantities. They are commonly used in the Indian spice mixture garam masala.

Coriander Seeds and Fresh Leaves
(Indian name – Dhania)

Leaves and seeds from the plant *Coriandrum sativam* are used extensively in Indian cooking. The fresh coriander leaves are also known as cilantro or Chinese parsley. They are believed to be world's most popular herb and are widely available in supermarkets in the United States. In Indian cuisine, cilantro is used as a garnish, as a flavoring agent and as one of the main ingredients in green chutney, a dipping sauce served with Indian snacks. Seeds from the coriander plant are used whole, crushed or ground. Ground coriander generally forms the largest component for most curry powders and the spices added to dishes for flavoring.

Cumin
(Indian name – Jeera)

A relative of the caraway seed, cumin seeds grow on a plant called *Cuminum cyaminum*. These brown seeds are used extensively—whole or in powder form—in Indian dishes. Whole seeds are usually roasted and crushed before use. Cumin must be subjected to heat before it will impart its flavor.

Curry Leaves
(Indian name – Kari Patta)

These are leaves from a small tree that grows wild all over India, and in North India, where I grew up, children used to identify this tree as Meetha Neem. The leaves have a strong aroma and flavor and are used frequently in South Indian dishes. Fresh curry leaves can be found in Indian grocery stores but are difficult to find elsewhere. They can be omitted from recipes in this book if they are not available.

Daal

Daal is an Indian word used for a variety of small beans, legumes and lentils. A large percentage of Indians are vegetarian, and daals are an important source of protein in their daily diet. Varieties of beans generally used in India include arhar (pigeon peas), chana (yellow split peas), moong (green gram), masoor (pink lentils), and urid (black gram). Daals are cooked whole, husked or husked and split in two. Flavored in a variety of seasonings, daals make a very desirable part of Indian vegetarian meals.

Fennel/Anise
(Indian name – Saunf)

Closely related, both these seeds are referred to by the same name in India. Fennel and anise have a sharp, sweet, minty flavor. The anise seeds, stronger in flavor, are smaller and crescent shaped. Fennel seeds are milder and larger. Powdered seeds are used in many dishes, especially in South India. Whole seeds are included in a mixture called panch poran in Bengal, and are used in many other dishes in this state. Whole seeds are consumed in many parts of India at the end of the meal as a kind of after-dinner mint.

Fenugreek Seeds and Leaves
(Indian name – Methi)

Leaves and seeds from the plant *Trigonella foenumgracum* are native to India. Both the leaves and seeds have a distinctive aroma and a pronounced bitter flavor, which mellows after cooking and becomes very pleasant. Fresh fenugreek leaves may be available in the summer in Indian grocery stores. Dried fenugreek leaves (called "Kasoori Methi") as well as fenugreek seeds are available year-round. Most of the recipes that use fenugreek herb in this book are made with the dried herb.

Garam Masala

Garam masala, a blend of a few aromatic spices, is used all over India. The exact recipe varies from cook to cook. Every cook likes to prepare his or her own blend of spices and call it garam masala. Some of the ingredients commonly used for garam masala are cardamoms, cloves, and cinnamon. In addition, peppercorns, cumin, coriander seeds, nutmeg and mace may also be added. The spices used for the blend are roasted whole and then ground up. Garam masala is best prepared fresh and used quickly, as the stored spice mixture loses its potent aromatic quality in a few days. My own version of garam masala is given below.

Recipe for Garam Masala

Roast in a skillet a mixture of the following:
  1 tablespoon whole cardamom
  1 tablespoon cloves
  One 2- to 3-inch stick cinnamon, broken into
      3 or 4 pieces
  1 tablespoon peppercorns
  A few blades of mace
Roast until the spices become slightly brown and emit a strong aroma, then transfer to a spice grinder and grind fine. Add a few shavings of nutmeg. Store in a tightly covered jar and use as soon as possible.

Ginger Root and Ginger Powder

Fresh ginger root should not need any introduction to western palates. Fresh ginger root is readily available, and peeled, finely chopped ginger is generally used in Indian cooking. Some recipes require ginger powder. You can find ginger powder in grocery stores everywhere.

Kewda or Kewra

Kewda is used to impart a flowery, perfume-like scent to dishes, usually desserts. Available in Indian stores as Ruh Kewda (essence) or kewda water, this fragrant water is made from flowers and petal-like leaves of the tropical screw pine plant *Pandanus tectorius* native to South India and Asia. Used in small quantities, kewda imparts an exotic fragrance to sweet dishes or rice pilafs.

Mace
(Indian name – Javitri)

Another exotic spice, mace is made from orange-red petals that grow around nutmeg fruit on the nutmeg tree *Myristica fragrans*. Mace is dried and sold as blades or ground up as powder. Many chefs add mace in small quantities to garam masala.

Mango Powder
(Indian name – Amchoor)

As the name suggests, this spice is powdered dried mango, made from the unripe mango. Added in small quantities, mango powder imparts a fruity sourness to the dishes. It is used primarily in North India.

Mustard Seeds, black
(Indian name – Rai)

These tiny, round, purplish-brown seeds come from an Indian mustard plant called *Brassica juncea*. They are milder than the yellow mustard seeds that are commonly used in the United States. When used in recipes, they are almost always added to hot oil as one of the first steps in cooking. Used this way, they pop and sputter, then turn gray and develop a nutty taste. Black mustard seeds provide a textural quality to the sauces or dishes.

Nigella Seeds
(Indian name – Kalonji)

These tiny, teardrop-shaped black seeds are obtained from the plant *Nigella sativa*. Also known as black onion seeds, they are not really related to onions. They are used in cooking just like black mustard seeds and impart a slightly peppery flavor and textural contrast to sauces and dishes.

Nutmeg
(Indian name – Jaiphal)

Nutmeg is the dried fruit of the nutmeg tree, which when dried is a hard, oval-shaped nut. Nutmeg is usually added to garam masala and used to provide an exotic fragrance to sweet dishes. Powdered nutmeg loses its potency very quickly, so it is best to store nutmeg whole and grate the amount you want to use as you need it.

Paneer Cheese

When I was growing up in India, the only cheese eaten in most of India was a freshly made cheese called paneer. It is a white, soft, creamy cheese with a sweet smell, generally made by most families at home by simply curdling boiled milk with whey and straining the milk solids. The strained cheese, wrapped in the straining cloth, is left under some heavy object (usually a pot filled with water) to squeeze out most of the moisture. Pressed paneer cheese is cut into cubes and used in many dishes. In vegetarian diets for many Indians, paneer cheese is an important source of protein.

Paprika

Made by grinding dried, ripe, sweet red chile peppers, paprika is commonly available in the United States and is used quite frequently in North India as well. A variety of paprika called deghi mirch is very popular in Kashmir and is used to impart a bright red color to sauces.

Peppercorns
(Indian name –Kali Mirch)

Peppers also are commonly used in the United States as well as India. Peppers grow on a vine, *Piper nigram*, native to India and they grow in abundance along the southwestern coast. Peppers are used in the green, berry form (available preserved in brine), in dried form (black peppercorn), or as white peppers. For white peppers, the berries are allowed to ripen on the vine. The outer skin is removed after the peppers are harvested, and the peppers are then dried.

Peppers should be ground fresh as they are used. The aroma and flavor of freshly ground pepper deteriorates very quickly. You probably have already invested in a good-quality peppermill; if not, you will want to do so.

Pomegranate Seeds, dried
(Indian name – Anardana)

Seeds from the pomegranate fruit are dried and used whole or in powder form to impart a very distinct sweet-sour flavor to food. They are common in some North Indian snacks (such as Pakoras and Alu Tikki) and breads (such as Paratha).

Poppy Seeds, white
(Indian name – Khaskhas)

The ripe seeds of the poppy plant *Papaver somniferum* used in India are white and are smaller than the gray seeds used in the United States, although they taste about the same. Poppy seeds are often used as a thickener for sauces and to impart a nutty flavor, mostly in North Indian dishes.

Rose Water
(Indian name – Gulab Jal)

Made from the petals of highly fragrant roses, rose water is an important addition to many sweet dishes from North India and Bengal. Rose water is readily available in bottles in Indian grocery stores. A more concentrated form, rose essence, is also available. When using essence, use only a few drops.

Saffron
(Indian name – Keshar)

Saffron is made from stigmas of the saffron crocus grown in Kashmir, China, the Mediterranean, and Asia Minor. The stigmas are pulled by hand from individual flowers. For this reason, the spice is very expensive. Fortunately, only a few threads of saffron are needed to infuse a dish with a warm, heady perfume and a beautiful light-orange color.

Tamarind
(Indian name – Imli)

Commonly used as a souring agent in curries (especially in South India) and in chutneys, tamarind is a fruit from the tree *Tamarindus indica*, which is native to India. The tamarind pods on the tree are covered with a brown shell, which is removed and discarded. The pulp of the tamarind is dissolved in water by mashing with your fingers, and the liquid is then strained for use, while the pith, seeds and fiber are discarded.

Several recipes in this book require use of tamarind concentrate, which can be prepared as follows:

Recipe for Tamarind Concentrate

Soak a 2 x 2 x 1-inch piece of tamarind pulp in 5 ounces warm water for about 1/2 hour. Mash tamarind between your fingers to thoroughly dissolve tamarind in the water. Strain through a sieve and discard seeds, pith and fibers. The strained tamarind liquid should now be as thick as buttermilk. Stir in 1/4 teaspoon salt. This concentrate can be prepared fresh when needed. Or you can prepare it ahead of time and freeze it in an ice cube tray. When needed, thaw out one ice cube at a time to use in the recipes.

Turmeric
(Indian name – Haldi)

Turmeric is a rhizome from the plant *Curuma longa*, which grows in India and southeast Asia. Turmeric is most commonly used as powder. This spice is responsible for the characteristic yellow color of Indian curries. It is used all over India and is almost indispensable in Indian cooking.

Samosas with Mint Cilantro Chutney

Pairing Wines with Indian Food

Ajanta is one of my favorite restaurants—not just my favorite Indian restaurant, but one of those special places where I seek a special dining experience. When Lachu asked me to write this chapter, I was quite honored. I have been an avid wine collector for over twenty years and few things give me more pleasure then sharing a fine meal with a well paired wine. Over the past dozen years, or so, Lachu and I have tasted, debated, discussed, and enjoyed many fine wines with his dishes. I am quite excited about sharing what we have learned.

—Aaron Moore,
Food and Wine Writer

Complex Food, Simple Wines

In general, the complex and layered flavors of Indian cuisine pair best with simple and straightforward wines. A fiery Goanese chicken curry will not showcase that special bottle of fine Burgundy or Bordeaux in its best light. In fact, a crisp white wine such as a Chenin Blanc, Riesling, Pinot Grigio, or Champagne will offer a much more refreshing foil against the heat and spice of that curry and many other lively Indian dishes. Red wines can also be very appropriate with your Indian meals. Seek out light to medium-bodied, fruity wines with a bit of acidity and low tannins—these lighter red wines will complement the flavors of the food and heighten the entire dining experience. For a hearty lamb korma or South Indian lamb curry, a light and lively Pinot Noir, juicy Côte du Rhone, or other Grenache-based wine would balance and blend much better than a heavy Cabernet, Merlot, or rich, jammy Zinfandel.

Big Is Bad

Big, extracted wines, meant for aging, are usually too much competition for the subtleties and spice of Indian dishes. The rich, concentrated flavors and firm tannins simply overwhelm the palate, instead of harmonizing with the food. Another issue against pairing big wines with Indian food is alcohol. Simply put, alcohol tastes "hot" and when combined with the spicy heat of a dish, wines with a lot of alcohol can taste even hotter. The heavy oak flavors often associated with new world Chardonnay and Cabernet can also compete unfavorably with Indian dishes. The layers of spice and nuance, so carefully nurtured in this complex cuisine, are erased by the monolithic oak character of these powerfully rich wines.

Moving beyond Gewürztraminer

With its lively, atypical fruit, low alcohol, and crisp acidity, wines made from Gewürztraminer grapes have long been considered to be one of the few "appropriate" pairings to the spicy and exotic cuisines of India and Asia. They are a suggestion perpetuated by countless restaurateurs, over the decades. While it is absolutely true that the racy spice and lively "bite" of these wines can be a wonderful accompaniment to similarly flavored foods, the pairing is somewhat limited.

Gewürztraminer is no more the "only" wine to serve with Indian food than Chianti is the only wine to have with pizza. Gewürztraminer, with its bold yet balanced character, is a particularly good match to a spicy prawn Masala, Tandoori chicken, or fish. Pairing such a distinctive wine with an appropriate course in your Indian feast can be quite a sensational part of the meal.

Perhaps, a Refreshing White to Tame the Spice

Besides the above-mentioned Gewürztraminer, countless other white wines will work as well. A crisp Sauvignon Blanc matches extremely well with any lightly herbal dish, including Tandoori asparagus, Kozi Milagu chicken, and appetizers served with the cilantro, mint, and tamarind sauce. The wonderfully fragrant and lightly sweet Riesling and Viognier wines match well with such dishes as chicken Mulligatawney, Machi Malai Masala, and fishcakes. Chardonnay can also be enjoyable, if you seek out one with little or no oak in its profile. Though uncommon in California, such low-oaked wines abound in the Burgundy region of France. The cuisine-conscious French appreciate these inexpensive whites for their clean, bright character of apple and melon flavors that become accessible when unburdened of the heavy vanilla notes imparted by too much oak. These wines are usually fermented in stainless steel and have limited barrel-time in which to absorb the oak. This style is often the most suitable Chardonnay to pair with a creamy, mild Indian dish such as Paneer Kofta.

One of the very best wine pairings with the lively spice of Indian cuisine is Chenin Blanc. The oft-maligned grape of jug-wine days is actually a highly regarded varietal that produces a dry wine of remarkable richness and versatility. Planted extensively in the Loire region of France, Vouvray, Samur, and Anjou are all stellar examples of Chenin Blanc. California also produces several serious examples of this varietal that are widely available. All of these Chenin Blanc wines have great, apple and melon flavors, good depth, balance, and enough crispness to stand up to the spice and heat of even the bolder Indian dishes. It is particularly good paired with Navataran Korma and Samosa.

Italian whites are also often quite agreeable with Indian dishes. Most are light, clean, and bright in flavor, with decent acidity and a touch of fruity sweetness. Pinot Grigio, Orvieto, and Malvasia are fairly ubiquitous in most wine shops. If you are inclined to seek out some of the less common gems, Tocai Friulano, Greco di Tufo, and Falanghina are particularly wonderful pairings. Among the white wines produced in Spain, Albariño would be an excellent match for an Indian meal. Fresh and vibrant, Albariño is often compared to a combination of

Sauvignon Blanc and dry Riesling. The fruity flavors are reminiscent of peaches, apricots, and melon, with tangy, bright overtones of citrus and spice—a perfect complement for such seafood delicacies as crab cakes and fish dishes.

Or Maybe a Red, Instead

Many of the bolder dishes described in this book will shine when accompanied by a generous, fruity red wine. The wines of the Rhône, with their juicy, bright cherry and plum flavors match nicely with everything from Tandoori chicken and Tamil lamb curry, to vegetarian preparation of Louts root and peas or other dishes cooked with a caramelized onion sauce. These red wines are often my first choice. Spanish red wines offer tremendous value these days, as well. Like their French counterparts, the Spaniards produce an abundance of medium-bodied wines slated for the table. These wines offer great depth of flavor and richness and are designed to pair with a wide range of bold cuisine. Rioja and Priorat are just two of this country's regions becoming more familiar to the American palate and with good reason. Their Tempranillo and Garnacha (Grenache) wines are ripe with rich, juicy plum and berry flavors, with hints of spice and woodsy nuance that marry well with many of the heartier dishes like Badal Jam and succulent Tandoori lamb chops.

The Australians also produce some very nice, lighter styled wines from Shiraz grapes (known as "syrah" in most other parts of the world). These wines bring a softer, ripe and candied expression of the grape than bolder versions from either France or California. The wines of California itself should not be forgotten. As with the whites, too much oak in red wine is the enemy. A medium-bodied Pinot Noir can be an ideal complement to a wide array of Indian dishes from chicken Tika Masala to a subtle lamb preparation such as Lamb Korma. For bolder fare (tandoori lamb or South Indian lamb curries, for example), seek out lighter versions of the classic Rhône varietals (Grenache, Syrah, and their blends), or a juicy, bright Sangiovese-based wine, such as a Chianti. Even Zinfandel will work, as long as it is lighter in style and has less than 14 percent alcohol.

Can't Decide on Red versus White? Consider Rose

If you are thinking I'm suggesting white Zinfandel, rest assured that I am not. There are many other suitable rosé wines to consider pairing with Indian dishes that are more then just simple, sweet, "pool-side" fun. Typically, white Zinfandel is too sweet and flabby to stand up to Indian dishes. Rosé wines, produced from other red varietals (such as Pinot Noir, Grenache, and Syrah), have the cool crispness to tame the flame of a searing Vindaloo, while also possessing some of the juicy, plump red wine characteristics demanded by Indian cuisine's bolder flavors. Lightly chilled, a good rosé from the south of France, Spain, or California will be a welcome match for many of the rich vegetarian, Biryani, and even fish dishes in this cookbook.

Break Out the Bubbly!

Another stellar wine, often overlooked as one to have with a meal, is Champagne. Champagne and other sparkling wines add a festive, celebratory note to any gathering. Their crisp, fruity balance matches perfectly with lightly fried Samosas, Pakora, and Alu Tiki appetizers. Although most often served before dinner, we have found that Champagne will complement most dishes, throughout the meal. Sparkling wines don't even have to be true Champagne (i.e., produced in the Champagne region of France) to merit consideration. Many countries produce countless sparkling wines of great quality at a very reasonable cost ($12 to $20). Some of the best are produced in France, outside of the Champagne region and are widely available at many wine stores.

Many of the well-known French Champagne producers have Californian properties, as well. Additionally, there are several homegrown wineries producing fabulous sparkling wines across the country. Even states not typically thought of as sources of fine wines, such as New York, Virginia, Missouri, and New Mexico, produce outstanding sparkling wines that are widely available and reasonably priced. Spain's Cava, and Italy's Prosecco are lovely, yet slightly sweet examples of how fun a bit of fizz can be. And while these expressions of sparkling wine definitely merit consideration, their inherent sweetness limits pairing them to desserts and the less-spicy dishes in Indian cuisine.

Indian Wines

Historically, wine has been produced and enjoyed in India since before the founding of the Moghul Empire. Early European visitors marveled at the quality of the wines produced in Hyderabad, Surat, and Maharashtra. At the Great Calcutta Exhibition of 1884 a large number of Indian wines were presented and well-received by the international crowd. In the late 1890s, Phylloxera decimated the Indian vineyards, as they had those in Europe and they hadn't begun to recover until almost one hundred years later.

Now, there is a bourgeoning Indian wine industry with the finest wines coming out of Karnataka and Sahyadri Hills in the state of Maharashtra. In 2004 and 2005 they produced some 300,000 cases with the majority of the wine being consumed locally. The three main exporting wineries are Indage, Grover, and Sula. Indage is a major producer of the award-winning sparkling wine Omar Khayam that is well worth

trying. Sula Vineyards is a very respectable producer of a full range of fine wines, including a sparkler, white Zinfandel, Chenin Blanc, Sauvignon Blanc, and Cabernet/Shiraz blend. The most impressive Indian wines I have sampled are those from Grover Vineyards. Grover Vineyards employed renowned wine consultant Michel Rolland to make their wines. His efforts have yielded an outstanding lineup. Among the best are his La Reserve red (Cabernet/Shiraz blend) that is rich and complex, and a most interesting white (a blend of Viognier and Clairette) that has an intriguing tangy finish, reminiscent of aged Parmesan cheese. Both of these wines are well worth finding.

I hope you enjoy the pleasure of fine wines paired with the excellent dishes you will discover in the pages of *Ajanta: Regional Feasts of India.*

Methi Murg (Chicken in Green Herb Sauce)

Feast from Kashmir

APPETIZER
Bhe' Ki Tikki (Lotus Root Cakes)

MAIN DISH
Methi Murg (Chicken in Green Herb Sauce)

SIDE DISH
Badal Jaam (Eggplant Topped with Tomato Sauce and Thickened Yogurt)

RICE DISH
Khumbi Pulav (Rice Pilaf with Mushrooms)

BREAD
Kashmiri Roti (Whole Wheat Flat Bread from Kashmir)

DESSERT
Firni (Rice Pudding)

KASHMIR, THE NORTHERNMOST STATE OF INDIA, is famous for its incredible beauty. Surrounded by towering snow-capped mountains of the Himalayan range, Kashmir is filled with gurgling streams, crystal-clear lakes and lush green valleys at six thousand feet above sea level. Visitors fondly talk about their stay in Kashmir, especially if the stay was on a houseboat. Typically, these houseboats are large enough to accommodate the owner's family as well as a visiting family. Included with the rooms are fabulous, unforgettable Kashmiri feasts prepared by the houseboat owners. The recipes in this chapter are for such a feast.

The cuisine of Kashmir shows two distinct culinary influences: Kashmiri Hindu Brahmins and Muslims. In contrast to Brahmins in the rest of the country, Kashmiri Brahmins eat lamb. Their cooking is characterized by the use of Kashmiri red chiles (called "deghi mirch"), fennel, ginger powder and asafetida. Brahmins frown upon the use of onions and garlic. A good example of the Kashmiri Brahmin cooking is the Kashmiri Rogan Josh, a lamb curry dish for which the sauce is prepared without using onions. Muslim cooking, on the other hand, freely uses onions and garlic. Influenced by visiting Moghul royalty, these dishes tend to be lavish, incorporating cream and other dairy products, nuts and exotic spices such as cardamom, cinnamon, cloves, mace and nutmeg. Since almost all the saffron used in the country is grown in Kashmir, it is liberally used by Kashmiris in their cooking.

Since Kashmir grows plenty of mushrooms, lotus root, green leafy vegetables and green herbs, these items are featured dominantly in their cuisine, as in the recipes here.

Bhe' Ki Tikki (Lotus Root Cakes)

Lotus root, one of my favorite vegetables, grows abundantly in Kashmir. I like this vegetable for its texture—hard and crunchy, somewhere between bamboo shoots and water chestnuts. I also like its flavor nuances of artichoke and asparagus. Bhe' Ki Tikki will prove to be an unusual and exotic appetizer. Lotus root can generally be found in Chinese markets or specialty produce stores.

INGREDIENTS (Serves 6)

1/2 pound lotus root

3 medium red potatoes, boiled, peeled and mashed (about 1 1/2 cups mashed)

3 slices white bread, crust removed, chopped into bread crumbs in a food processor

1/4 cup loosely packed chopped fresh dill

1 teaspoon salt

1 teaspoon crushed chile pepper

1 1/2 teaspoons crushed dried pomegranate seeds

1 teaspoon black cumin seeds

2-inch piece fresh ginger, peeled and chopped fine

Oil for pan frying

1. Cut lotus root near root ends or joints. Discard joints or root ends. Cut lotus root into 2-inch-long pieces. Scrub or peel outer skin; clean dirt from holes if necessary. Boil for 1 1/2 hours, or until the lotus root is tender. Cool and cut into a fine dice, 1/8 to 1/4 inch in size.

2. Mix diced lotus root with the rest of the ingredients except oil. Divide into eight to twelve portions and form each portion into a round, smooth cake, about 2 inches in diameter.

3. Heat oil (about 1/4 inch deep) in a large skillet. When the oil is hot, almost to the smoking point, drop 2 to 3 cakes in the oil. Fry on each side for about 2 minutes, until crispy and brown. Remove and place in a tray lined with paper towels. Repeat until all cakes are fried, adding more oil as necessary. Frying too many cakes at one time will reduce the oil's temperature; the cakes will fall apart and soak up too much oil. Serve with Yogurt Mint Cilantro Chutney.

Yogurt Mint Cilantro Chutney

1 large tomato, cored and coarsely chopped

1/2 medium onion, peeled and coarsely chopped

2 cups loosely packed cilantro, with stems and roots discarded

1 cup loosely packed mint leaves

1 green chile pepper (serrano or jalapeño), chopped (optional)

1/2 teaspoon salt

3 to 4 teaspoons Tamarind Concentrate (see page 26)

1/2 cup plain yogurt

Puree all ingredients except yogurt together in a blender. The blending process will be easier if items with more moisture—tomato and onion—are pureed first. Transfer to a bowl and mix in yogurt. Taste and add more salt and tamarind if needed.

This can be made ahead of time and stored in the refrigerator for up to 3 days.

Bhe' Ki Tikki (Lotus Root Cakes)

Methi Murg (Chicken in Green Herb Sauce)

The sauce in this dish is not the familiar yellow or orange curry sauce. The use of herbs makes it green. I like the sauce for its fresh herbaceous aroma and intriguing flavors. Every time we feature this dish at Ajanta, customers rave about it.

INGREDIENTS (Serves 6)

1/4 cup oil

1-inch piece ginger, peeled and finely chopped

8 cloves garlic, peeled and chopped

1/2 to 2 green serrano or jalapeño chiles, to taste, chopped

3 medium onions, peeled, cut in quarters and thinly sliced

2 pounds deboned and skinned chicken leg meat (approximately 7 legs), cut into 1- to 2-inch pieces

1 1/2 cups loosely packed chopped cilantro

1/2 cup loosely packed chopped dill

4 tablespoons dry fenugreek herb

2 teaspoons turmeric

2 medium tomatoes, pureed

1 cup plain yogurt

1 1/2 teaspoons salt

1 teaspoon Garam Masala (see page 24)

1. Heat the oil in a 6- to 8-quart nonstick saucepot. When hot, add ginger, garlic and chiles. The oil should be hot enough so the ginger and garlic sizzle when added. Sauté for 10 to 15 seconds. Add onions and sauté over medium-high heat for 10 to 12 minutes, or until lightly brown, stirring about every 2 minutes.

2. Raise heat to high. Add chicken and stir occasionally until chicken is browned, about 5 to 7 minutes. Continue this process until most of the moisture in the pot has evaporated.

3. Add the remaining ingredients except Garam Masala. Bring to a boil, reduce heat, cover and simmer over low to medium heat for about 20 minutes, or until the chicken is tender. Add Garam Masala; mix and remove from heat.

Badal Jaam (Sliced Eggplants Topped with Tomato Sauce and Thickened Yogurt)

In my experience, I have not come across any eggplant dish that tastes as good as this one. This is the only vegetarian dish that has remained on the Ajanta menu continually, due to its enormous popularity. It is an elaborate dish, requiring many steps, but the result makes it worth all the time spent in preparing it.

INGREDIENTS (Serves 6)

2 cups plain yogurt

2 tablespoons lemon juice

10 medium cloves garlic, peeled and finely minced

1/2 teaspoon salt

1/4 cup chopped fresh cilantro, divided

2 large globe eggplants, cut into 3/4-inch-thick slices

1 1/2 teaspoons salt

Oil for pan frying

1 tablespoon oil

1-inch piece ginger, peeled and chopped

6 to 8 cloves garlic, peeled and chopped

1/2 medium onion, peeled and chopped

2 teaspoons paprika

1 teaspoon salt

4 medium tomatoes, coarsely chopped and pureed in a food processor

1 1/2 teaspoons each: toasted powdered cumin seeds, black salt powder, mango powder and chile flakes

1. Hang yogurt in a muslin cloth over the sink and let the whey (water) drip out for about 2 hours. Transfer the thickened yogurt to a bowl and add lemon juice, garlic, 1/2 teaspoon salt and half of the cilantro. Mix thoroughly and set aside.

2. Salt eggplant slices with 1 1/2 teaspoons salt and let drain for about 30 to 45 minutes. Pat dry. Heat oil in a 10-inch skillet (about 1/4 inch deep) and fry eggplant slices over medium to high heat until golden brown, about 3 to 4 minutes on each side. Remove and let drain on paper towels. Set aside.

3. Heat 1 tablespoon oil in a 4-quart saucepan. When hot, add ginger and garlic and sauté for 20 seconds. Add chopped onion and sauté over medium heat until soft, about 6 to 8 minutes. Add paprika, 1 teaspoon salt

and tomatoes; simmer for 30 to 40 minutes, or until the sauce becomes thick and is the consistency of ketchup.

4. Place eggplant slices in a deep baking tray in a single layer. Generously brush the top of each eggplant slice with the tomato sauce. Mix together cumin, black salt, mango powder and chile flakes, and sprinkle on top of the eggplant slices. Seal the tray tight with aluminum foil. Bake in a preheated oven for 20 minutes at 275 degrees F.

5. Serve with a dollop of thickened yogurt sauce and a sprinkle of the remaining chopped cilantro on each slice.

Badal Jaam (Sliced Eggplant Topped with Tomato Sauce and Thickened Yogurt)

Khumbi Pulav (Rice Pilaf with Mushrooms)

This is a variation on a well-known Kashmiri dish called Guchi Pulav, which is made with morel mushrooms. Morels are hard to find and very expensive. If you wish to use them, by all means, do so. Alternatively, use a mushroom of your choice. I have experimented with various mushrooms and like shiitakes best in this recipe, even though they are not Indian. I also highly recommend the optional use of chicken broth. The rice takes on a light brown color and flavor from the caramelized onions, making them visually appealing as well as very flavorful. This is one of my favorite rice dishes. For entertaining friends at home, I have cooked Khumbi Pulav more often than any other rice dish.

INGREDIENTS (Serves 6)

3 tablespoons oil

1 medium onion, peeled, cut into quarters and thinly sliced

1 cup shiitake mushroom caps, sliced 1/4 to 1/2 inch thick

2 cups basmati rice

4 cups chicken broth or water

6 bay leaves

3 sticks cinnamon

1 1/2 teaspoons salt, or to taste

1. Heat the oil in a 6- to 8-quart saucepot. Add onion and sauté until dark brown. It is important to make sure the onion is caramelized nicely so that the rice picks up the brown color and caramelized flavor.

2. Add mushrooms and sauté for 2 minutes. Add rice and stir-fry for 3 to 4 minutes. Stir-frying rice prior to adding liquid seals in the starch, and the rice, when cooked, will not stick together.

3. Add water or chicken broth, bay leaves, cinnamon sticks and salt. Bring to a boil, reduce heat, cover and simmer for 15 to 20 minutes, or until the rice is cooked and all the liquid has been absorbed. Fluff rice with a fork.

Kashmiri Roti (Whole Wheat Flat Bread from Kashmir)

Roti, a whole wheat bread found all over India, is made in many versions. Kashmiri roti is distinguished by its use of milk and various spices in the dough. In addition, the Kashmiri rotis are griddle-fried with a small amount of oil. This makes the rotis richer than rotis made in the rest of northern India.

INGREDIENTS (Serves 6)

2 cups chapati flour or other low-gluten, whole-wheat, pastry-grind flour

1/2 teaspoon salt

2 to 3 tablespoons oil

1/2 teaspoon anise seeds

1/2 teaspoon cumin seeds

1 teaspoon black pepper powder

1/2 teaspoon ajwain

1/4 teaspoon asafetida

3/4 cup (approximately) warm milk

Oil for griddle frying

1. To make the dough, mix all the ingredients except milk and oil for frying, in a large bowl, baking pan, or food processor. Add milk gradually, working it into the flour, mixing and kneading. Use it gradually and use only the amount of milk necessary to make a fairly stiff dough. The exact quantity will vary depending on the type of flour used. Form the dough into a flattened ball, cover with a damp towel, and let sit for about 1 hour.

2. Heat a griddle on high heat. Turn the heat down to medium once the griddle is hot.

3. Divide the dough into ten portions. Form each portion into a small ball by rolling it between your palms. Flatten balls, dust with a little flour and roll them out with a rolling pin into circles about 1/16 to 1/8 inch thick. (See process photos on facing page.)

4. Cook rolled-out rotis on the griddle for about 30 to 40 seconds on each side, or until they look slightly golden brown. Then smear or spread 1/3 tablespoon of oil on the top surface of each roti using the back of a tablespoon. Flip the roti and fry until crisp and golden brown, about 30 seconds. Repeat on the other side.

Making Whole Wheat Flat Bread from Kashmir

Firni (Rice Pudding)

Firni is a variation on Kheer, or traditional Indian rice pudding that is popular all over the country. Firni is made with ground rice rather than the whole rice used in Kheer. I prefer making Firni with coarsely ground rice rather than rice flour, as is traditionally done in Kashmir.

INGREDIENTS (Serves 6)

1/4 cup + 2 tablespoons ground rice

4 cups milk

Seeds from 7 cardamom pods

1/2 cup sugar

1 large pinch saffron

1 tablespoon each: slivered almonds, chopped pistachios and raisins

1 tablespoon kewda water

1. In a spice or coffee grinder, coarsely grind rice by pulsing for a couple of seconds a few times. Stop grinding when it looks like most rice kernels are broken up in 2 or 3 pieces. The rice will not be broken up uniformly—some of the rice might even be powdered, while other pieces stay intact. That is okay. Set aside.

2. In a 4- to 6-quart saucepot, bring milk to a boil. Stir frequently using a wire whisk to dislodge any milk solids that might stick to the bottom. When milk starts to boil, reduce heat to medium. Simmer at medium heat, stirring, until the milk is reduced to 3/4 of its original volume. This should take about 20 minutes. Add cardamom seeds. Do not remove from heat; continue to simmer gently at low heat.

3. Add crushed rice to the milk and continue to simmer for about 25 minutes, stirring frequently with a wire whisk to make sure that there are no lumps.

4. Add sugar and stir to dissolve. Mix in saffron and simmer for another 2 minutes. Taste to adjust sweetness and to make sure that the rice is cooked and soft. If rice is not soft, continue cooking for a few more minutes. Add almonds, pistachios, raisins and kewda water. Serve warm in small bowls. (If cooked earlier, warm before serving.)

FROM YOUR REFRIGERATOR AND PANTRY

Ginger	4-inch piece
Garlic	26 cloves
Oil	
Sugar	3/4 cup
Milk	3 quarts
Raisins	1 tablespoon
Almonds	1 tablespoon
Pistachios	1 tablespoon
Salt	

FROM YOUR INDIAN SPICE RACK

Turmeric	2 teaspoons
Paprika	2 teaspoons
Cumin seeds	2 teaspoons
Black cumin seeds	1 teaspoon
Cardamoms	7 pods
Cinnamon sticks	3
Saffron	A large pinch
Ajwain seeds	1 teaspoon
Asafetida powder	1/4 teaspoon
Black pepper powder	1 teaspoon
Crushed chile pepper	2 1/2 teaspoons
Bay leaves	6
Garam Masala	1 teaspoon
Dried pomegranate seeds, crushed	1 1/2 teaspoons
Anise seeds	1/2 teaspoon
Black salt powder	1 1/2 teaspoons
Dried fenugreek herb	4 tablespoons
Tamarind	1 tablespoon
Kewda water	
Mango Powder	1 1/2 teaspoons

SUPERMARKET SHOPPING LIST

Red potatoes	1 1/2 pounds
Onions	6 medium
Tomatoes	8 medium
Cilantro	3 bunches
Lotus root	1/2 pound
Shiitake mushrooms	1/2 pound
Mint	1 bunch
Green chile peppers	2
Fresh dill	1 bunch
Lemons	1
Eggplant, round	2 large
Yogurt	2-pound tub
Whipping cream	1 cup
Chicken broth	4 cups
White bread	4 slices
Chicken, 7 whole legs	About 3 1/2 pounds

SPECIALTY SHOPPING

Basmati rice	2 1/2 cups
Chapati flour	2 1/2+ cups

Chicken Makhanwala (Tandoori Chicken Breasts in Creamy Curry Sauce)

Feast from Punjab

THE STATE OF PUNJAB IS IN NORTHERN INDIA, just south of Kashmir, and shares its western border with Pakistan. The state derives its name from five rivers flowing through it. The word *punjab* is composed of two words: *punj*, meaning "five," and *aab*, meaning "water." These rivers make Punjab one of the most fertile states in India. With the abundance of grains, produce, milk and dairy products, Punjabis tend to be robust and hearty eaters.

Punjabi cuisine is earthy, zesty and filling. Butter, ghee and other milk products are used generously in Punjabi cuisine. The base sauce for cooking includes ginger, garlic, onions and tomatoes, flavored with ground dry spices. Tandoori cooking is usually associated with Punjabi cooking. With wheat being the staple crop in Punjab, breads made with wheat (roti, naan and parathas) are preferred over rice. Over time, Punjabi cuisine incorporated external influences, primarily Moghul, giving it a dimension that made it so appealing that Punjabi cooking became very popular all over India. Today, Punjabi restaurants and Punjabi dishes can be found in every state in India.

Punjabi cuisine and tandoori cooking have been made famous by Punjabi chefs throughout the world. In the United States, Punjabis own more Indian restaurants than any other Indian ethnic group. Many of the Punjabi dishes are so popular that they are offered as menu items by most Indian restaurants in the country. These include tandoori chicken, chicken makhanwala, shish kabobs, saag gosht, baingan bharta, saag paneer, matar paneer, malai kofta and dal makhani.

Khumb Alu Tikki (Potato Cakes Stuffed with Mushrooms)

Alu tikki, cakes made with boiled potatoes and usually stuffed with curried peas, are very popular not only in Punjab but in most North Indian states. In many regions, the cakes are flavored with spices unique to the region. Indians love Alu tikkis, and at Ajanta, Alu Tikki has always been a very popular appetizer. I am surprised to notice that not many Indian restaurants in the United States feature this item.

The recipe here is a variation on the traditional recipe. This filling is made with mushrooms instead of peas, but if you prefer peas to mushrooms, feel free to substitute.

INGREDIENTS (Serves 6)

2 tablespoons oil

1/3 pound mushrooms (shiitakes recommended), stems removed, cut into 1/4-inch dice

2 to 3 medium red potatoes, boiled, peeled and mashed (about 1 1/2 cups mashed)

2 slices white bread, crust removed, processed into bread crumbs in a food processor

1-inch piece ginger, peeled and finely diced

2 teaspoons dried pomegranate seed powder

1/2 cup loosely packed chopped cilantro

1 1/2 teaspoons salt

1 teaspoon chile flakes

1 green chile pepper, finely chopped (optional)

Oil for pan frying

1. Heat the 2 tablespoons oil in a frying pan. Add mushrooms, then stir and sauté for about 5 minutes. Set aside.

2. In a bowl, thoroughly mix all the ingredients except oil and mushrooms. Divide in six equal portions. Form each portion into a round patty about 1/2 inch thick. Put 1 heaping tablespoon of sautéed mushrooms in the center of the patty. Close the patty around the mushrooms. Re-flatten into the

shape of a round cake, about 3/4 inch thick.

3. Heat oil at least 1/4 inch deep in a skillet. When hot to about 375 degrees F, fry 2 to 3 cakes at a time until crispy, about 2 to 3 minutes on each side. Frying too many cakes at one time will reduce the temperature of the oil and the cakes will fall apart and soak up too much oil. Replenish the oil as necessary. Drain fried cakes on a paper towel. The cakes are best served soon after frying. Cook this item just before guests start to arrive, and serve with Mint Cilantro Chutney.

Mint Cilantro Chutney

Mint Cilantro Chutney is like a thick dipping sauce. About 2 tablespoons of sauce should usually be served with each Alu tikki. The recipe gives more than needed for the appetizer for six. The remaining amount can be used as a dipping sauce with other appetizers or served as a side with dinner.

INGREDIENTS

2 to 3 tablespoons tamarind concentrate (see step 1 below for instructions)

1 large tomato, coarsely chopped

1/2 medium onion, coarsely chopped

2 cups loosely packed cilantro (about 1 bunch), thick stems removed
1/2 cup mint leaves (about 1/2 bunch)

1 green serrano chile pepper, about 3 inches long, chopped (optional)

1/2 teaspoon salt

1. Make the tamarind concentrate by soaking a large lemon-size ball of tamarind in a small bowl for 1 hour in enough water to cover. Mash with fingers to dissolve. Strain. The final concentrate should be the consistency of thick buttermilk.

2. Puree all ingredients together in a blender. The blender will work better if moist ingredients (tamarind concentrate, tomato and onion) are pureed first. Taste and adjust for salt and tamarind.

Khumb Alu Tikki (Potato Cakes Stuffed with Mushrooms)

Chicken Makhanwala (Tandoori Chicken Breasts in Creamy Curry Sauce)

A classic Indian dish, this is one of the recipes that is featured on the menu at most Indian restaurants in India as well as in the United States. Makhan means "butter" in the Hindi language, and for this reason many chefs add large amounts of butter to the sauce of this dish. The real meaning of makhanwala in this recipe is that the sauce is "smooth like butter." The recipe below has some cream in the sauce, and when properly cooked, the sauce becomes smooth like butter, without being very rich and without the use of butter.

INGREDIENTS (Serves 6)

Tandoori Chicken:

2 lemons

3 teaspoons salt

6 chicken breasts, boned and skinned

MARINADE:

2 shallots, peeled and minced

1 cup yogurt

8 to 10 cloves garlic, peeled and finely minced

2-inch piece ginger, peeled and finely minced

3 teaspoons paprika

1 teaspoon Garam Masala (see page 24)

1 1/2 tablespoons oil

Makhanwala Sauce:

2 tablespoons oil

6 cloves of garlic, peeled and chopped

2-inch piece ginger, peeled and finely chopped

9 medium tomatoes, pureed

1 green chile pepper, stem removed, chopped

1 tablespoon dried fenugreek herb

2 teaspoons salt

2 teaspoons turmeric

4 teaspoons paprika

1/2 to 2 teaspoons hot chile pepper powder

2 teaspoons cumin powder

1/2 cup yogurt

3/4 cup heavy cream

2 teaspoons Garam Masala (see page 24)

Tandoori Chicken:

1. Cut lemons in half. Place 2 teaspoons salt on a shallow plate. Dip 1/2 lemon in salt; squeeze the lemon, applying juice and salt to the chicken breasts. Continue until all the chicken breasts are covered with salt and lemon juice. Set aside for about 30 minutes.

2. Prepare marinade by mixing together all of the marinade ingredients. Generously coat the chicken breasts with marinade and refrigerate 24 hours or overnight. Bring to room temperature before cooking.

3. Preheat broiler in the oven. Place marinated chicken on a roasting rack so the chicken is exposed to the heat from all sides. Place the rack in the oven about 8 inches below the broiler. Place aluminum foil under the rack to catch the drippings. Broil the chicken for 8 minutes. Turn over the breasts and broil on the other side for 5 minutes. It is okay if the breasts are slightly undercooked at this time, since they will simmer in the Makhanwala sauce later. Allow to cool and then cut each breast into four pieces.

Makhanwala Sauce:

1. Heat the oil in a 6- to 8-quart saucepot. When hot, add garlic and ginger. Oil should be so hot that ginger and garlic sizzle when added. Sauté for about 10 seconds.

2. Add pureed tomatoes, green chile pepper, fenugreek herb, salt and all the spices except garam masala. Simmer, partially covered, over low to medium heat until the sauce becomes quite thick. Whisk in yogurt and cream.

Putting it all together:

1. Add chicken breasts and simmer, uncovered, over low to medium heat for 10 minutes. Add Garam Masala and cook 2 minutes more. Check to see that the chicken is cooked through and tender. When done, the sauce should be thick enough to coat the back of a spoon, about the consistency of buttermilk. If the sauce is too thick, add some water during cooking. If the sauce is too thin, remove all the chicken with a slotted spoon and reduce the sauce by boiling until it reaches the desired consistency. Return chicken to the pan.

Baingan Bharta (Pureed Roasted Eggplant with Onions, Tomatoes and Spices)

This is another classic dish that appears on the menu at most Indian restaurants. Lovers of Indian food everywhere seem to know this dish by name and love it for its smoky flavor, acquired by flame-roasting the eggplants. Flame-roasting as shown in this recipe requires cleaning the burners after, but the exceptional flavor is worth the extra effort.

INGREDIENTS (Serves 6)

2 large round eggplants, about 1 pound each

6 tablespoons oil

2 teaspoons cumin seeds

2-inch piece of ginger, peeled and finely chopped

1 hot green chile (serrano or jalapeño), chopped (optional)

3 medium onions, peeled and chopped

6 medium tomatoes, chopped

4 teaspoons paprika

1/2 to 1 teaspoon cayenne powder

2 teaspoons turmeric

2 teaspoons coriander powder

2 teaspoons salt

1/4 cup chopped cilantro

1. Roast eggplants on the open flame of a gas burner. This is best done with prongs over a medium flame. Place an eggplant on each burner and turn them about a quarter turn every 30 seconds or so. The outside skin of the eggplants will become charred and juices will ooze out. Continue to roast until the eggplants become soft, about 15 to 20 minutes, depending on the size of the burner. Cook the stem end longer than the blossom end. The charred skin gives the eggplants a nice smoky flavor. The eggplant is done when a fork pierces it easily.

Alternately, eggplant can be roasted in a 450 degree F oven for about 45 to 50 minutes. Oven-roasting is easier, but the eggplant will not have much of a smoky flavor.

Remove and let the eggplants cool. Peel and discard the stalk and skin. Coarsely chop the eggplant pulp, chopping the harder portions more fine. Reserve.

2. In a sauté pan, heat the oil over high heat. When hot, add cumin seeds (oil should be hot enough that it sizzles when seeds are added; test by dropping a couple of seeds in first), and fry for about 10 seconds. Add ginger and green chiles, and sauté for 10 seconds. Add onions and sauté for about 8 to 10 minutes over medium to high heat, stirring every 2 minutes, or until the onions are translucent. Add chopped tomatoes and cook, uncovered, for 5 minutes. Add the spices and salt. Simmer over medium to low heat for another 15 minutes, partially covered (or with lid removed if the sauce is too watery), stirring every 2 to 3 minutes, until the mixture is quite thick. The finished sauce should be the consistency of yogurt.

3. Add the chopped eggplant and cook, partially covered, over medium heat for about 8 to 10 minutes, stirring occasionally. Remove from heat and sprinkle cilantro on top.

Baingan Bharta (Pureed Roasted Eggplant with Onions, Tomatoes and Spices)

Haldi Chaval (Rice with Turmeric and Green Onions)

INGREDIENTS (Serves 6)

2 tablespoons oil

8 green onions, thinly sliced (separate white and green parts)

2 cups basmati rice

4 cups water

1/2 teaspoon turmeric

1 1/2 teaspoons salt, or to taste

1. Heat the oil in a 6- to 8-quart saucepot. Add the white parts of the onions and sauté for 3 to 4 minutes. Add rice and sauté over medium-high heat until rice begins to turn opaque, about 3 to 5 minutes, stirring frequently. This step will seal in the starch so the rice will not stick together when it is cooked.

2. Add water, turmeric and salt. Bring to a boil, reduce heat, cover and simmer until all the moisture is absorbed, about 20 to 25 minutes. Remove from heat. Fluff rice with a fork and sprinkle green parts of the onions on top. The cooked rice should have a very pleasant light-yellow color, dotted with bright green onions.

Parathas (Griddle-Fried Layered Flat Bread)

This whole wheat bread is popular not only in Punjab but throughout India. It is made in many variations and is often served at breakfast. Paratha, stuffed with a mixture of ajwain seeds and crushed chile peppers, served with some homemade full-fat yogurt is one of my favorite breakfasts.

INGREDIENTS (Serves 6)

2 cups chapati flour or other whole-wheat, low-gluten, pastry-grind flour

3 tablespoons oil

1/2 teaspoon salt

3/4 to 1 cup water

Flour for dusting

1/2 cup oil or ghee (clarified butter) for frying

1. Mix the flour with oil and salt. Add water gradually, working it into the flour, mixing and kneading. Use only the amount of water necessary to make the dough. Knead the dough well until it is supple and elastic. Store in a bowl covered with a damp cloth for 30 minutes to 1 hour.

2. Heat a griddle on high heat. Turn to medium once the griddle is hot.

3. Divide the dough into eight portions. Form each portion into a small round ball by kneading it between your palms. Flatten the ball and dust it with a little flour, then use a rolling pin to roll it out into a circle less than 1/8 inch thick. Smear oil or ghee on top of the rolled-out dough; fold into a half-circle. Smear more oil or ghee on the folded dough, and fold once more into a quarter-circle. Dust more flour on the folded paratha and roll it out again to less than 1/8 inch thick. The rolled-out paratha will not be a circle. (See process photos on page 56.)

4. Cook the rolled-out paratha on the griddle for about 30 to 40 seconds on each side. Smear the top side with oil or ghee and flip to fry. Repeat this procedure on the other side. The cooked paratha should have golden-brown spots. Transfer to a serving plate. Repeat the baking and frying process until all the parathas are done.

Aam di Kulfi (Mango, Milk and Cream Frozen Dessert)

Aam di Kulfi (Mango, Milk and Cream Frozen Deʌʌert)

Kulfi, prepared in many variations, is as popular among children and adults in India as ice cream is in the United States. Having grown up in India, I have fond memories of running out and buying kulfi popsicles whenever the kulfi cart wandered into the neighborhood.

INGREDIENTS (Servea 6)

1/2 gallon half-and-half

Seeds from 6 to 8 cardamom pods

1/3 to 1/2 cup sugar

1 1/2 cups mango puree

1. In a thick-bottomed 6- to 8-quart saucepot, bring half-and-half to a boil over high or medium–high heat. Stir once every minute or so with a wire whisk, dislodging any milk solids that might stick to the bottom of the pot, and preventing the milk from getting a burnt flavor. Add cardamom seeds during this time.

2. Once the milk starts to boil, reduce heat to medium and continue cooking for 1 to 1 1/2 hours, stirring every 3 minutes or so. Let thicken until it is reduced to about a third of its original volume. Check the volume by dipping a wooden spoon in the milk and measuring the height before and after thickening. At this time, the reduced liquid should have a consistency of thick buttermilk.

3. Add 1/3 cup sugar and stir to dissolve. Let cool. Add pureed mangoes. Taste and adjust for sweetness by adding more sugar if necessary. Pour the thickened milk-and-mango mixture into six ramekins. Freeze the kulfis.

4. To soften the kulfis for serving, transfer them to the refrigerator about 30 minutes before serving. Serve in the ramekins or transfer to a plate by holding the ramekin on its side in running water and then turning it upside down on a serving plate. Cut into 6 slivers.

Making Griddle-Fried Layered Flat Bread

FROM YOUR REFRIGERATOR AND PANTRY

Ginger	7 inch piece
Garlic	16 cloves
Sugar	1/2 cup
White bread	2 slices
Butter	1/2 stick
Oil	
Salt	

FROM YOUR INDIAN SPICE RACK

Turmeric	4 1/2 teaspoons
Paprika	11 teaspoons
Coriander powder	2 teaspoons
Cumin powder	2 teaspoons
Cumin seeds	4 teaspoons
Cardamoms	8 pods
Crushed chile pepper /chile flakes	1 1/2 teaspoons
Garam masala	3 teaspoons
Dried pomegranate seeds, crushed	2 teaspoons
Dried fenugreek herb	1 teaspoon
Hot chile pepper powder	3 teaspoons

SUPERMARKET SHOPPING LIST

Red potatoes	3 medium
Onions	4 medium
Tomatoes	17 medium
Cilantro	2 bunches
Mushrooms (Shiitake recommended)	1/3 pound
Mint	1 bunch
Green chile peppers	4
Lemons	2
Eggplant, round, large	2
Yogurt	2 cup
Whipping cream	1 cup
Chicken breasts,	6
Shallots	2
Green onions	8
Half-and-half	1/2 gallon

SPECIALTY SHOPPING

Basmati rice	2 cups
Chapati flour (Can substitute low-gluten, pastry-grind whole-wheat flour)	2 cups
Canned mango puree (Or equivalent fresh mangoes)	1 can (1 1/2 cups needed)
Tamarind Concentrate	2 x 2-inch piece

Seyal Machi (Fish in Caramelized Onion Sauce)

Feast from Sindh

SINDH DOES NOT EXIST AS A STATE in India anymore. This state was converted to Pakistan when British rule ended in India in 1947. Sindhi culture, however, is very much alive and well. Almost all Hindu Sindhis migrated to India, while Muslim Sindhis stayed in Pakistan. The majority of Hindu Sindhis are now settled in Bombay and in parts of Rajasthan. The Sindhi language is one of the eighteen officially recognized regional languages of India and has its own script.

Sindhis are well known for their love of the finer things in life. This is also true of their cuisine, which tends to be rich. Cooking vegetables by deep-frying till they are caramelized is a common practice among Sindhis and is one of the distinguishing features of Sindhi cuisine. Sindhis use a variety of souring agents to a great extent in their cooking, more so than most North Indian cuisines. These include mango powder, tamarind, kokum flowers and dried pomegranate seeds. Sindhi cuisine is influenced by Punjab and Gujarat, both of these states being close to Sindh (when it existed). Gujarati influence is evidenced by the use of mustard seeds, fenugreek seeds and asafetida. Punjabi influence, on the other hand, is indicated by the extensive practice of sautéing vegetables as opposed to boiling or steaming them.

I am a Sindhi, and all the dishes included in this chapter are family recipes and are some of my favorites.

Sanha Pakoras (Chickpea-Flour Fritters)

Pakoras, or chickpeas fritters, are very popular all over India and most regions have their own version. Usually Pakoras are made by dipping slices of potatoes or other vegetables in a batter made with chickpea flour (called besan *in Hindi) and then deep-frying them. Chickpea-flour batter is often flavored with spices, which may include turmeric, chile flakes, cumin powder, ajwain or other spices. At times, some rice flour or baking powder is added to the batter to make the pakoras crispier.*

Sindhi Sanha Pakoras are different from pakoras made in other parts of India. Onions and potatoes are finely diced and mixed with many other ingredients, such as ginger, chile peppers, cilantro and pomegranate seeds. The result, in my very biased opinion, is pakoras that taste better than any other.

INGREDIENTS (Serves 6)

1 cup chickpea flour	1 teaspoon salt
1/2 cup finely chopped onion	1-inch piece ginger, finely diced
1/2 cup finely diced potatoes (1/8- to 1/4-inch dice)	1/2 teaspoon baking powder
	1 teaspoon chile flakes
1 tablespoon dry pomegranate seeds, coarsely pounded	1/4 cup loosely packed chopped cilantro
1 tablespoon coriander seeds, coarsely pounded	Oil for deep-frying

1. Mix all the ingredients except oil and add just enough water to make a thick paste.

2. Heat the oil in a 6- to 8-quart saucepot. Using a large spoon, drop several large dollops (2 to 3 inches in diameter) of the paste into the hot oil and deep-fry to a golden brown at medium to high heat. Frying too many pakoras at one time will reduce the temperature of the oil and the pakoras will fall apart and soak up too much oil. Remove and place in a tray or platter lined with paper towels. Repeat until the entire mixture is finished.

3. Break up the fritters into about 1-inch pieces, and fry these pieces one more time at high heat to a crispy, dark golden-brown color. Remove and place on another platter lined with paper towels. Serve with Mint Cilantro Chutney (see page 47).

Sanha Pakoras (Chickpea-Flour Fritters)

Seyal Machi (Fiʌh in Caramelized Onion Sauce)

This seafood dish is very popular at Ajanta and is often requested for an encore. Seyal Machi has an unusual, thick sauce made with caramelized onions. Spices cooked with caramelized onions take on a smoky flavor, since there is no moisture. The sourness of the mango powder, one of the spices used in the sauce, plays nicely against the sweetness of the caramelized onion.

INGREDIENTS (Serveʌ 6)

6 tablespoons oil, divided	2 teaspoons paprika
4 medium onions peeled and cut into 1/8-inch dice	1/2 to 2 teaspoons hot chile pepper powder
4 teaspoons coriander powder	2 teaspoons salt
1 1/2 teaspoons turmeric	2 pounds catfish fillets (or other white fish like halibut or snapper), cut into 2- to 3-inch pieces
2 teaspoons mango powder	

1. In a 6- to 8-quart saucepot, heat about 4 tablespoons of oil. Add onions and sauté over high heat, stirring frequently, until the onions are deep golden brown, almost caramelized. Heat should be kept high enough so the onions dehydrate and do not become soggy.

2. Add all the spices and salt. Lower the heat a little bit. Stir and cook for about 5 minutes. Reduce to low heat, and leave the sauce on low until the next step is done.

3. In another 10- to 12-inch sauté pan, heat the remaining oil until it becomes very hot, almost to the point of smoking. While the oil is getting hot, pat dry the pieces of fish in a clean towel. Sauté the fish in the hot oil about 30 seconds on each side, until it changes color. Transfer the fish to the pot with the sauce. Raise to medium heat and cook until the fish is cooked through and flakes easily, about 3 to 4 minutes. The cooking time will depend on the thickness of the fish pieces. Reduce the cooking time for thinner pieces.

Alu Aur Sem Ki Fali (Green Beans with Potatoes)

This simple dish has become my wife's favorite since it is so easy to prepare and is very tasty. It's a good example of how I generally like to cook vegetables, by dehydrating them instead of boiling them. This is done by sautéing them in oil in a skillet. This method of cooking by dehydrating concentrates the flavor of vegetables. (See photo page 2.)

INGREDIENTS (Serves 6)

3 tablespoons oil

6 to 8 cloves garlic, peeled and chopped

1 pound green beans, ends trimmed, cut in 2-inch pieces

1 large potato, peeled, halved and cut in 1/8-inch-thick slices

1 teaspoon turmeric

3 teaspoons coriander powder

1 teaspoon paprika

1/2 to 2 teaspoons hot chile pepper powder

1 teaspoon mango powder

1 teaspoon salt

1. Heat the oil in a medium or large saucepan or sauté pan. Sauté chopped garlic for about 15 seconds or until slightly golden brown.

2. Add beans and potato slices. Stir and sauté for 10 to 12 minutes.

3. Add remaining ingredients. Mix and cook, uncovered, over medium-high heat for 5 to 10 minutes, until beans and potatoes are cooked. Stir every 2 to 3 minutes.

Sindhi Khichree (Rice with Mung Beans)

INGREDIENTS (Serves 6)

1 tablespoon oil	4 cups water
2 teaspoons black cumin seeds	1/2 cup mung beans, split
2 cups basmati rice	1 1/2 teaspoons salt

1. Heat the oil in a 6- to 8-quart saucepot. When hot, add black cumin seeds (oil should be hot enough to sizzle when seeds are added; test by dropping a couple of seeds in first) and fry for 10 seconds.

2. Add rice. Sauté for 3 to 4 minutes, until the rice starts to change color and becomes opaque. Add water, mung beans and salt. Bring to a boil and then turn down the heat; cover and simmer until all the liquid is absorbed, about 20 minutes. Remove from heat and fluff rice with a fork.

Sindhi Fulka (Sindh Whole Wheat Flat Bread)

INGREDIENTS (Serves 6)

2 cups chapati flour or other low-gluten, whole-wheat, pastry-grind flour

1/2 teaspoon salt

2 tablespoons oil

Oil or melted butter for brushing bread

3/4 cup plus 2 tablespoons water

Flour for dusting

1. Mix all the ingredients except oil for brushing, water, and flour for dusting in a large bowl or baking pan. Add water gradually, working it into the flour, mixing and kneading. Do not use all the water at once; add it gradually and use only what is necessary. Knead the dough until it is supple and elastic. The exact quantity of water will vary depending on the type of flour used. Form the dough into a flattened ball; cover with a damp towel and let sit for about 30 minutes.

2. Heat a griddle on high heat, then turn down to medium.

3. Divide the dough into about ten portions. Form each portion into a small ball. Flatten the ball, dust with a little flour, and roll it out on a flat surface to about 1/4 inch thick in a long, oval shape. Smear about 1/2 teaspoon oil or melted butter on the top surface. Pinch the oval in the center, and fold one side over the other. Press the two sides of the oval together, dust both sides with a small amount of dry flour and, using a rolling pin, roll it out into a circle about 1/16 inch thick. (See process photos on page 68.)

4. Bake rolled-out fulka on the griddle for about 30 to 40 seconds on each side. The fulka will puff up and have golden-brown spots. Brush it with a small amount of oil or butter, and save in a basket or plate lined with paper towels. Repeat steps 3 and 4 for the remaining balls of dough. It is best to prepare the fulkas just before sitting down to eat.

Gajar Halva (Carrot Pudding with Nuts)

Gajar Halva (Carrot Pudding with Nuts)

You might not think of a carrot dessert as being something special, but this is undeniably one of the best Indian desserts.

INGREDIENTS (Serves 6)

3/4 pound carrots, peeled and grated

1 1/2 quarts whole milk

1 1/2 sticks sweet, unsalted butter

3/4 cup sugar

Seeds from 8 cardamom pods

1/4 cup (total) slivered almonds and pistachio pieces

1. In a saucepot, combine carrots and milk. Bring to a boil, whisking frequently with a wire whisk to make sure that the milk does not stick to the bottom of the pan. Cook the mixture over medium heat for about 1 hour, or until it becomes thick. Continue stirring frequently to avoid a burnt flavor.

2. Add butter, sugar and cardamom seeds, and continue to cook until the mixture becomes thick enough to draw away from the sides and bottom of the pot in a semi-solid mass. This might take another 30 minutes to 1 hour. The cooking time will be more if you are scaling up the recipe.

3. Transfer halva to a serving platter and decorate the top with the almond and pistachio mixture.

 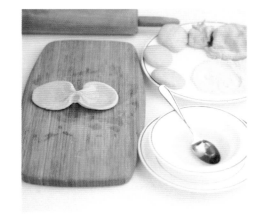 

Making Sindh Whole Wheat Flat Bread

68

Sindh Feast Shopping List

FROM YOUR REFRIGERATOR AND PANTRY

Ginger	1 inch piece
Garlic	8 cloves
Sugar	3/4 cup
Whole milk	1 1/2 quarts
Sweet, unsalted butter	2 sticks
Almonds, slivered	1/8 cup
Pistachios, pieces	1/8 cup
Baking powder	1/2 teaspoon
Oil	
Salt	

FROM YOUR INDIAN SPICE RACK

Turmeric	2 1/2 teaspoons
Paprika	3 teaspoons
Coriander powder	7 teaspoons
Mango powder	3 teaspoons
Hot chile pepper powder	4 teaspoons
Crushed chile pepper/chile flakes	1 teaspoon
Coriander seeds	1 tablespoon
Black cumin seeds	2 teaspoons
Cardamoms	8 pods
Dried pomegranate seeds, crushed	1 tablespoon

SUPERMARKET SHOPPING LIST

Red potatoes	3 medium
Onions	6 medium
Tomatoes	1 large
Carrots	3/4 pound
Cilantro	1 1/2 bunches
Mint leaves	1/2 bunch
Green chile pepper	1
Green beans	1 pound
Catfish (or other whitefish) fillets	2 pounds

SPECIALTY SHOPPING

Basmati rice	2 1/2 cups
chapati flour (Can substitute low-gluten, whole-wheat, pastry-grind flour)	2 1/2 cups
Chickpea flour	1 cup
Mung beans, split	1/2 cup
Tamarind Concentrate	2 x 2-inch piece

Murgi Ka Saalan (Chicken Curry)

Non-Vegetarian Feast from
Uttar Pradesh

IF INDIAN FOOD WERE CATEGORIZED into two major general categories, these would be North Indian and South Indian. There are many common features in food from most North Indian states and the same can be said about the food from most states in South India. North India is dominated by a state called Uttar Pradesh, *uttar* being the Indian word for "north." In the United States, more restaurants serve North Indian food than serve South Indian food. The same is true for Indian cookbooks sold in the U.S.

The following recipes incorporate characteristics generally associated with North Indian food from the state of Uttar Pradesh, which is distinguished by the sauces based on onions or tomatoes or a combination of both. These may be flavored with ginger, garlic, yogurt, lemon juice and variety of spices including turmeric, coriander, cumin, chile peppers, cardamom, cinnamon and cloves.

Mixed Vegetable Pakoras (Sliced Vegetable Fritters)

Pakoras, made by frying slices of vegetables (most commonly potatoes) dipped in chickpea batter, are one of the most commonly served appetizers in North India. Indians almost always have a frying pan filled with oil (called kadhai) ready by the side of the range. At a moment's notice, Indian homemakers can whip up chickpea batter, slice some vegetables, and fry and serve a very satisfying dish of hot pakoras to a hungry household.

INGREDIENTS (Serves 6)

Vegetables: cut in thin slices (1/8 inch)

1 medium potato, peeled, cut in half, and sliced

1 Chinese eggplant, about 8 inches long, sliced (stem removed)

2 zucchini, ends trimmed, sliced

1 teaspoon salt

Batter:

1 cup loosely packed chickpea flour

1 teaspoon baking powder

1 teaspoon ajwain seeds

1/2 teaspoon salt

1/2 teaspoon chile flakes

1/2 cup water

Oil for deep-frying

1. Sprinkle sliced vegetables with 1 teaspoon salt and set aside in a colander for about 30 minutes to get rid of excess moisture. Pat dry with a paper towel.

2. Prepare the batter by mixing all the ingredients together with a wire whisk, being sure to beat out all lumps.

3. Heat oil to 325 to 350 degrees F in a pot for deep-frying. When hot, dip sliced vegetables in the batter, and then deep-fry at medium to high heat. If the batter is too thin and does not stick to the slices, mix in more chickpea flour (about 1 tablespoon) to thicken the batter. Fry 8 to 10 pakoras at a time. Frying too many at one time will reduce the temperature of the oil and the pakoras will soak

up too much of it. Frying may take about 6 to 8 minutes per batch. Turn and fry pakoras on both sides, as needed, so they are crispy and golden brown. Remove and drain on a plate lined with paper towels. Serve hot with Sweet-and-Sour Tamarind Chutney.

Sweet-and-Sour Tamarind Chutney

Small piece tamarind pulp (2 × 2 × 1 inch)

3/4 cup warm water

1/4 teaspoon salt

1 teaspoon crushed chile peppers

2 teaspoons sugar

Soak tamarind pulp in warm water for about 30 minutes. Mash tamarind between your fingers to thoroughly dissolve in the water. Strain through a sieve, and discard seeds, pith and fibers. The strained tamarind liquid should be as thick as buttermilk. Add remaining ingredients and mix.

Mixed Vegetable Pakoras (Sliced Vegetable Fritters)

Murgi Ka Saalan (Chicken Curry)

I am very fond of this recipe. During my first few months in the United States, when I started to cook for myself, this was the first recipe I perfected.

INGREDIENTS (Serves 6)

3 tablespoons oil

6 to 8 medium cloves garlic, finely chopped

3 to 4 medium onions, cut in 6 wedges along the length and sliced 1/16 inch thick

2 pounds deboned and skinned chicken dark meat, cut in 1- to 2-inch pieces

3 teaspoons cumin powder

1/2 to 1 1/2 teaspoons hot chile pepper powder

2 teaspoons turmeric

1 teaspoon paprika

1 1/2 teaspoons Garam Masala (see page 24)

1 1/2 teaspoons salt, or to taste

2 medium tomatoes, pureed

1 cup plain yogurt

1/2 cup chopped cilantro

1. Heat the oil in a 6-quart saucepan. When hot, add chopped garlic and sauté for about 10 seconds (garlic should sizzle when dropped in oil). Add onions and cook over medium-high heat, stirring occasionally, for 10 to 12 minutes, or until the onions become soft and slightly golden brown.

2. Raise to high heat. Add chicken and sauté until it is nicely browned, about 4 to 5 minutes. At this time, if there seems to be too much moisture, continue to sauté and stir until most of the moisture has evaporated.

3. Add all the spices and salt. Mix and stir-fry for about 2 to 3 minutes. Add and mix pureed tomatoes. Turn down heat, and mix in the yogurt. Raise the heat again. Bring the mixture to a boil, reduce heat and simmer, covered (but vented), for about 15 to 20 minutes, or until chicken becomes tender. The finished curry should have a consistency of thick buttermilk. If the sauce is too watery, remove the lid and boil off some of the water. If the sauce is too thick, add some water (about 1/4 cup) and mix.

4. Stir in cilantro, then remove from heat.

Methi Wala Alu Gobhi Matar (Potatoes, Peas and Cauliflower with Fenugreek)

One of the popular dishes that appears on the menu of most Indian restaurants in the United States is a vegetarian dish called Alu Gobhi. Literally translated, alu gobhi means "potatoes and cauliflower." The recipe below is a variation on alu gobhi. It includes green peas and has a sauce flavored with my favorite herb, fenugreek.

INGREDIENTS (Serves 6)

1/4 cup oil

6 to 8 cloves garlic, chopped

1-inch piece ginger, peeled and chopped

2 medium onions, chopped

3 medium tomatoes, chopped

2 teaspoons cumin powder

2 teaspoons hot chile pepper powder (substitute all or part with paprika to make the dish mild)

3 teaspoons coriander powder

1 1/2 teaspoons turmeric

1 1/2 teaspoons salt, or to taste

3 tablespoons dried fenugreek herb

2 medium potatoes, peeled and cubed into 1-inch pieces

1 1/2 pounds cauliflower, cut into florets

1/2 cup shelled fresh peas or frozen peas

2 tablespoons lemon juice

1. Heat the oil in a 6-quart saucepan. When hot, add garlic and ginger. Fry for about 10 to 15 seconds. Add onions and sauté for about 8 to 10 minutes over medium to high heat, stirring once every 2 to 3 minutes.

2. Add chopped tomatoes. Stir and cook for about 5 minutes. Add and mix all the spices, salt and dried fenugreek. Stir and cook for another 2 to 3 minutes.

3. Add potatoes, mix, and cook partially covered for 7 to 8 minutes, stirring every 2 to 3 minutes. Add cauliflower and fresh peas (if using frozen peas, add later, during last 4 minutes of cooking). Mix and cook, covered, over medium heat for about 20 minutes, stirring every 3 to 4 minutes. If there is too much moisture, cook with lid removed. If there is too little moisture and the vegetables start to stick to the bottom of the pot, cover and reduce the heat. Continue to cook until vegetables are tender.

4. Add lemon juice. Mix and cook another 2 minutes.

Methi Wala Alu Gobhi Matar (Potatoes, Peas and Cauliflower with Fenugreek)

Zaffrani Chaval (Rice with Saffron and Nuts)

INGREDIENTS (Serves 6)

1 tablespoon oil	1 1/2 teaspoons salt
1 teaspoon black cumin seeds	Pinch saffron
2 cups basmati rice	2 tablespoons warm water
4 cups chicken broth or water	1/3 cup pine nuts or cashew nuts

1. Heat the oil in a 6-quart saucepan. When hot, add black cumin seeds (oil should be hot enough to sizzle when seeds are added; test by dropping a couple of seeds in first) and stir for 10 seconds.

2. Add rice. Stir and sauté for 3 to 4 minutes. The rice will start to change color and become opaque. Add broth or water and salt. Bring to a boil, turn down heat, cover and simmer until all the liquid is absorbed, about 20 minutes. Turn off heat and fluff rice with a fork.

3. Dissolve saffron in 2 tablespoons of warm water, then pour it in the center of rice. Sprinkle nuts on top. Wait for 5 minutes and then mix. Rice will have white and saffron-color grains mixed together, which look very pretty.

Naan (Flat Bread Made with Leavened Dough)

Naan is undeniably the most popular Indian bread. In restaurants, naan is always cooked in a tandoor oven, a clay-lined, charcoal-fired, cylindrical or conical oven that runs very hot, usually at a temperature exceeding 700 degrees. The recipe shown here uses a broiler in a home oven.

INGREDIENTS (Serves 6)

4 cups loosely packed white flour	1/2 teaspoon salt
1 1/2 teaspoons active dry yeast mixed in	1/2 cup plain yogurt
1/4 cup warm water	3/4 cup water (approximately)
3 tablespoons oil	Flour for dusting
1 egg	Melted butter for brushing cooked naan

1. Put flour in a large bowl. Add yeast, oil, egg, salt and yogurt and mix thoroughly. Add water gradually, working it into the flour, mixing and kneading. Do not use all the water at once; add it gradually and use only what is necessary. Knead the dough well until it is supple and elastic. The exact quantity of water will vary depending on the type of flour used and how accurately it was measured. Place dough in a large nonreactive bowl. The bowl should have enough room for dough to rise. Leave covered and let rise for about 4 to 6 hours.

2. Divide dough into eight to ten equal parts, then form each into a round ball; leave on a tray or baking sheet, loosely covered with plastic wrap, to rise a second time for 3 to 4 hours.

3. Turn on the oven broiler and let it heat for about 30 minutes. Flatten each dough ball, dust with flour, and with a rolling pin, roll into an oval shape. The rolled-out naan should be about 1/8 inch thick. Place on a baking sheet and set it under the broiler for 30 to 40 seconds, or until the top surface of the naan becomes lightly golden brown. Remove tray from the oven, turn the naan over, and cook it on the other side for about 20 seconds. The second side should be just cooked, not golden brown. Remove from the broiler and brush with melted butter on the brown side. Repeat until all the naan are cooked.

Making Naan (Flat Bread Made with Leavened Dough)

Keshar Pistachio Kulfi (Ice Cream–Like Dessert Flavored with Saffron and Pistachios)

The mere mention of kulfi makes Indians salivate. Kulfi is made in many northern states with varying flavors. The recipe shown below, flavored with saffron and pistachios, is a delicious version.

INGREDIENTS (Serves 6)

1 gallon half-and-half	1/2 cup chopped pistachios
Seeds from 8 to 10 cardamom pods	1/2 teaspoon saffron
1 to 1 1/4 cups sugar, or to taste	3 tablespoons kewda water

1. In a thick 6- to 8-quart saucepot, bring half-and-half to a boil over medium to high heat. To prevent half-and-half from getting a burnt flavor, stir once every minute or so with a wire whisk, scraping the bottom to dislodge any milk solids. Add cardamom seeds during this time. Once mixture starts boiling, reduce to medium heat and continue to thicken it, stirring once every 5 minutes or so until the milk is reduced to about a third of its original volume. This might take about 2 hours at medium heat. Check the volume by dipping a ruler or wooden spoon in the milk and measuring the height before and after thickening.

2. Add sugar and stir to dissolve. Add and mix pistachios and saffron. Let cool. Add kewda water. Pour about 4 ounces each of mixture into small ramekins. Freeze at least 3 hours.

3. Transfer the kulfis to the refrigerator about 30 minutes before serving to soften them. Unmold kulfis by inverting ramekins onto serving plates. Sprinkle additional chopped pistachios on top, if desired.

Uttar Pradesh Feast Shopping List

FROM YOUR REFRIGERATOR AND PANTRY

Ginger	1 inch piece
Garlic	16 cloves
Oil	
Sugar	1 1/2 cups
Pistachios, chopped	1/2 cup
Cashews or pine nuts	1/3 cup
Salt	
Baking powder	1 teaspoon
White flour, all-purpose	4 1/2 cups
Active dry yeast	1 1/2 teaspoons
Egg	1 large
Butter (For brushing on bread)	1/4 stick

FROM YOUR INDIAN SPICE RACK

Turmeric	3 1/2 teaspoons
Paprika	3 teaspoons
Coriander powder	3 teaspoons
Cumin powder	5 teaspoons
Hot chile pepper powder	3 1/2 teaspoons
Crushed chile pepper/ Chile flakes	1 1/2 teaspoons
Black cumin seeds	1 teaspoon
Ajwain seeds	1 teaspoon
Cardamoms	10 pods
Saffron	1/2 teaspoon
Garam Masala	1 1/2 teaspoons
Dried fenugreek herb	3 tablespoons
Kewda water	3 tablespoons

SUPERMARKET SHOPPING LIST

Red potatoes	3
Onions	6 medium
Tomatoes	5 medium
Cilantro	1/2 bunch
Lemons	1
Cauliflower	1 large
Fresh shelled or frozen peas	1/2 cup
Chinese eggplant	1
Zucchini squash	2
Yogurt	1 1/2 cups
Chicken broth	4 cups
Chicken	7 whole legs (about 3 1/2 pounds)
Half-and-half	1 gallon

SPECIALTY SHOPPING

Basmati rice	2 cups
Chickpea flour	1 cup
Tamarind Concentrate	2 x 2-inch piece

Paneer Kofta (Paneer Cheese Balls in Curry Sauce)

Vegetarian Feast from
Uttar Pradesh

A LARGE PERCENTAGE OF THE POPULATION in India is vegetarian. Additionally, the nonvegetarians in India rarely eat meat every day. I grew up in a nonvegetarian family. It was not unusual for us to eat meat only two times a week. Therefore, vegetarian cooking and vegetarian dishes make up a majority of the meals consumed in India. For this reason, vegetarian cooking has evolved much more in India than in any other country. Indian vegetarian meals are nutritionally balanced, flavorful and very enjoyable. Dishes based in legumes, lentils or paneer cheese are usually part of the vegetarian meal, and these provide protein in the Indian vegetarian diet.

Samosas (Turnovers Stuffed with Potatoes and Peas)

Samosas are, without any doubt, the most popular appetizer in all Indian restaurants in the United States. In my years of restaurant ownership, I have yet to meet one person who does not like samosas. Serve samosas for your dinner party and you will start your evening on a very positive note. (See photo page 27.)

INGREDIENTS (Serves 6)

Dough:

1 cup loosely packed all-purpose flour

1/4 teaspoon salt

3 tablespoons oil

1teaspoon ajwain seeds

1/4 to 1/3 cup water

Potato Filling:

3 medium potatoes

2 tablespoons oil

1/2 cup frozen peas, thawed

1 teaspoon salt

2 teaspoons coarsely ground coriander seeds (grind coarsely in a spice grinder by pulsing a few times)

1 teaspoon chile flakes

1 teaspoon mango powder

1 teaspoon turmeric

Oil for deep-frying

1. Make the dough for samosas by mixing together flour, 1/4 teaspoon salt, 3 to 4 tablespoons of oil, ajwain seeds and water. Add water slowly while making the dough and use only the amount necessary. The dough should be fairly stiff. Knead dough for a few minutes, then cover with a damp towel and let rest for 30 minutes to 1 hour.

2. Boil potatoes. When done, peel the potatoes and cut into 1/4-inch dice. Heat 2 tablespoons oil in a large skillet. Add potatoes, peas, salt and all the spices. Mix and cook for 5 minutes. Let cool.

3. Divide the dough into six equal parts and the potato mixture into twelve equal parts. Form each part of the dough into a smooth ball by

squeezing between your palms; then roll it out in a circle about 7 to 8 inches in diameter. Cut the circle in half. Place one part of the potato mixture in the center of each half-circle. Wet the outside edges of the rolled-out samosa dough by dipping a finger in water and running it along the edges. Fold two sides of the half circle, one at a time, on top of the potato mixture, overlapping in such a way as to form a triangle. Press or pinch around the wet edges, making sure it is sealed thoroughly.

4. Heat oil to about 300 degrees F in a pot for deep-frying. Deep-fry 3 to 4 samosas over medium-low heat until they are golden brown, turning them to cook both sides equally. Maintain oil temperature at around 300 to 325 degrees F. Frying too many samosas at one time will reduce the temperature of the oil and the samosas will soak up too much oil. But allowing the oil to get too hot will brown the samosas on the outside before the crust is cooked through.

Serve with Mint Cilantro Chutney (see page 47).

Making Samosas (Turnovers Stuffed with Potatoes and Peas)

Paneer Kofta (Paneer Cheese Balls in Curry Sauce)

Kofta is an Indian word for balls made with vegetables or meat, usually served in a curry sauce. Indians are very fond of kofta dishes. Many versions, both vegetarian and nonvegetarian, are made all over India. Koftas made with paneer cheese, also known as Malai Kofta, are considered very desirable because paneer cheese is a good source of protein. This is an elaborate preparation, but the dish is worth all the trouble.

INGREDIENTS (Serves 6)

Curry Sauce:

3 tablespoons oil

6 cloves garlic, finely chopped

1 medium onion, cut into quarters and sliced very thin

2 teaspoons paprika

1/2 to 2 teaspoons hot chile pepper powder

3 teaspoons cumin powder

1 1/2 teaspoons turmeric powder

2 teaspoons salt

1 1/2 teaspoons Garam Masala (see page 24)

4 medium tomatoes, finely chopped

1 cup water

3/4 cup heavy cream

Paneer Cheese for Koftas:

1/2 gallon whole milk

1/3 cup white vinegar

Koftas:

3 medium red or yellow potatoes

3 slices white bread, crusts removed, processed into breadcrumbs

1 teaspoon salt

2 teaspoons powdered dry pomegranate seeds

1 1/2 teaspoons ajwain seeds

1 teaspoon chile flakes

1 tablespoon finely chopped chile pepper (optional)

1/4 cup loosely packed cilantro

Oil for deep-frying

Curry Sauce:

1. Heat oil in a 6- to 8-quart nonstick saucepot. When hot, add garlic and sauté for about 10 seconds. Oil should be hot enough so that the garlic sizzles when added. Add onion and sauté over medium to high heat,

stirring every minute or so, until translucent, about 8 to 10 minutes.

2. Add all the spices (except Garam Masala) and salt and sauté for about 3 to 5 minutes. Then add the chopped tomatoes and stir and sauté for about 5 minutes. Transfer to a food processor and coarsely grind the mixture by pulsing 5 to 6 times (this step is optional; when done, it results in a smooth, homogeneous sauce). Transfer mixture back to the pot and place over low to medium heat; add 1 cup water, cover and slowly simmer for 30 to 40 minutes, or until a sheen of oil is seen on the top. Check and stir every 5 minutes to make sure the sauce does not stick to the bottom of the pan. If that happens, reduce the heat slightly. The finished sauce should have a consistency of heavy cream. If the sauce is too thick, add some water. If it is too thin, remove the lid and boil off some of the liquid. Remove from heat and reserve.

3. Swirl in the cream and mix. Sprinkle Garam Masala on top.

Paneer cheese for koftas:

1. In a saucepan, bring milk to a boil. Stir in the white vinegar, then turn off the heat. The milk will curdle. Let it cool.

2. After about 20 minutes, strain the curdled milk through a piece of muslin. Squeeze off any excess moisture by twisting and wringing the cloth around the curds. Place the curds left in the cloth under a heavy pot filled with water or some other heavy object to squeeze out more moisture. Remove from under the weight after 40 minutes and crumble the paneer cheese.

Koftas:

1. Boil potatoes; when cooked, cool, peel and mash. Add crumbled paneer cheese, breadcrumbs, salt, spices and cilantro.

2. Divide potato mixture into twenty-four equal parts, and roll each part between your palms into a ball about 1 1/2 inch in diameter. (See process photos on page 90.) Deep-fry the balls 3 to 5 at a time. Be sure that the oil is very hot, otherwise the kofta balls will fall apart. Frying too many balls at one time will reduce the temperature of the oil and the balls will soak up too much oil and become heavy. Deep-frying is best done just before eating.

3. Just before serving, heat the Curry Sauce. Ladle some into a bowl or soup plate and place four kofta balls in the center.

Sabzi Rangarang (Mixed Vegetables in Spicy Sauce)

Sabzi Rangarang (Mixed Vegetables in Spicy Sauce)

Literally translated, the title of this dish means "vegetables of many colors." A poetic way of saying mixed vegetables.

INGREDIENTS (Serves 6)

1/3 cup oil

1 teaspoon mustard seeds

6 to 8 cloves garlic, chopped

1 green chile pepper, chopped (optional)

1-inch piece ginger, peeled and chopped

2 medium onions, finely chopped

3 teaspoons coriander powder

2 teaspoons mango powder

1 teaspoon turmeric

2 teaspoons cumin powder

2 teaspoons paprika

1/2 to 2 teaspoons hot chile pepper powder

2 teaspoons salt

3 medium tomatoes, chopped

2 medium potatoes, peeled and cut into 3/4-inch dice

2 carrots, cut in half lengthwise and then into 1/2-inch slices

1 1/2 pounds cauliflower, cut into small florets 1 inch in diameter

1/2 pound green beans, ends trimmed, cut into 1- to 2-inch pieces

1. Heat oil in a 6- to 8-quart saucepot. When hot, add mustard seeds. After the seeds pop, add garlic, green chile pepper and ginger. Stir for about 20 seconds. Add onions and sauté over medium–high heat until soft, about 8 to 10 minutes.

2. Add all the spices and salt. Sauté for 3 to 4 minutes. Add chopped tomatoes and cook the mixture over medium heat another 5 minutes.

3. Add potatoes and carrots. Stir and cook over medium heat for 10 minutes, stirring every 2 to 3 minutes. Add the remaining vegetables and cook over medium heat, partially covered, until the vegetables become soft, about 30 to 40 minutes. Stir every 4 to 5 minutes. Make sure the sauce does not stick to the bottom of the pan and burn. If sauce is too thick, add 2 to 4 tablespoons of water. If there is too much moisture, cook uncovered to dry out the mixture. The final dish should have a thick, almost dry sauce.

Making Paneer Kofta (Paneer Cheese Balls)

Zaffrani Chaval (Saffron Rice)

INGREDIENTS (Serves 6)

1 tablespoon oil	1 1/2 teaspoons salt
1 teaspoon black cumin seeds	Pinch saffron, steeped in 2 tablespoons warm water
2 cups basmati rice	
4 cups water	

1. Heat oil in a saucepot. When hot, add black cumin seeds (oil should be hot enough to sizzle when seeds are added; test by dropping a couple of seeds in first) and sauté for 10 seconds.

2. Add rice. Sauté for 3 to 4 minutes until rice starts to change color and becomes opaque. Add water and salt. Bring to a boil, turn down heat, cover and simmer for about 20 minutes, or until all the liquid is absorbed and the rice is cooked.

3. Pour saffron water in a 2-inch circle in the middle of the rice pot. Leave covered for about 5 minutes while the saffron water is absorbed. Fluff the rice with a fork and mix. The result should be a very pleasant-looking mixture of white and yellow grains.

Chapati (Whole Wheat Flat Bread)

Chapati is the most common and basic bread consumed in North India as well as in many other regions of the country. Made with whole wheat flour, this bread is light and nutritious.

INGREDIENTS (Serves 6)

2 cups chapati flour, or pastry-grind durum wheat flour

1/2 teaspoon salt

2 tablespoons oil

3/4 to 1 cup water

Flour for dusting

Melted butter for brushing on cooked bread

1. Mix all the ingredients except water in a large bowl or baking pan. Add water gradually, working it into the flour, mixing and kneading. Do not use all the water at once; add it gradually and use only what is necessary. Knead the dough well until it is supple and elastic. The exact quantity of water will vary depending on the type of flour used. Form dough into a flattened ball and cover it with a damp towel.

2. Heat a griddle on high. Turn the heat down to medium once the griddle is hot.

3. Divide dough into eight to ten portions and form each portion into a small round ball. Flatten balls, dust with a little flour and, with a rolling pin, roll them out on a flat surface in a circle about 1/16 inch thick.

4. Bake rolled-out chapatis on the griddle for about 30 to 40 seconds on each side; then, holding chapatis with a pair of tongs, place each on gas burner over a high flame for a few seconds on each side. The chapatis will puff up and have golden-brown spots. Brush chapatis with a small amount of butter or oil before serving.

Making Chapati (Whole Wheat Flat Bread)

Kheer (Indian Rice Pudding)

Not limited to North India, Kheer is cooked in almost all parts of the country. The flavoring used for Kheer differs from state to state and even from family to family. The version shown here is how I prefer to cook this wonderful dessert.

INGREDIENTS (Serves 6)

1 1/2 quarts milk

Seeds from 4 cardamom pods

6 tablespoons rice

1/2 cup plus 2 tablespoons sugar

1/3 cup mixture of raisins, slivered almonds and chopped pistachios

Large pinch saffron

1 tablespoon kewda water

1. In a thick 6- to 8-quart saucepot, bring milk to a boil over high or medium-high heat. Stir every minute or so with a wire whisk to dislodge any milk solids from the bottom of the pan to prevent a burnt flavor. Add cardamom seeds during this time. Once milk comes to a boil, reduce heat to medium and continue to thicken it, stirring every 5 minutes or so, for about 20 to 25 minutes.

2. Add rice and sugar. Cook, uncovered, over low heat, stirring occasionally, until the rice is cooked to a soft consistency, about 30 to 35 minutes. Add the raisins, nuts and saffron. Cool until it is slightly warm. Add the kewda water and serve.

Kheer (Indian Rice Pudding)

Vegetarian Feast Shopping List

FROM YOUR REFRIGERATOR AND PANTRY

Ginger	1 inch
Garlic	14 cloves
Oil	
Sugar	3/4 cup
Whole milk	1 gallon
Raisins	1/8 cup
Almonds	1/8 cup
Pistachios	1/8 cup
Salt	
White bread	3 slices
All-purpose flour	1 cup
Frozen peas	1/2 cup
White vinegar	1/3 cup
Butter	1/2 stick

FROM YOUR INDIAN SPICE RACK

Turmeric	3 1/2 teaspoons
Paprika	4 teaspoons
Coriander powder	3 teaspoons
Cumin powder	5 teaspoons
Mango powder	3 teaspoons
Hot chile pepper powder	4 teaspoons
Crushed chile pepper /Chile flakes	2 teaspoons
Cumin seeds	1 teaspoon
Coriander seeds	2 teaspoons
Black cumin seeds	1 teaspoon
Mustard seeds	1 teaspoon
Cardamoms	4 pods
Saffron	2 large pinch, about 1/2 teaspoon
Ajwain seeds	2 1/2 teaspoons
Garam Masala	1 1/2 teaspoons
Dried pomegranate seeds, crushed	2 teaspoons
Kewda water	1 tablespoon

SUPERMARKET SHOPPING LIST

Red potatoes	8 medium
Onions	4 medium
Tomatoes	9 medium
Cilantro	1 1/2 bunch
Mint	1/2 bunch
Carrots	2
Green chile peppers	3
Green beans	1/2 pounds
Cauliflower	1 large head
Whipping cream	3/4 cup

SPECIALTY SHOPPING

Basmati rice	2 cups + 6 tablespoons
Chapati flour (Can substitute low-gluten, pastry-grind, whole-wheat flour)	2 cups
Tamarind Concentrate	2 × 2-inch piece

Khumb Jahanara (Mushrooms with Creamed Spinach and Spices)

Moghlai Feast from North India

THE WORD MOGHLAI IS COMMONLY USED to describe a cuisine that evolved in North India as a result of Moghul influence on Indian cooking. Muslim royalty, who appreciated and became connoisseurs of complex Indian cuisine, promoted the art of cooking and hired talented chefs. Dishes were created to please kings and queens and were named after them. Since cost was no object, the dishes were elaborate and rich with exotic ingredients. This style of cuisine flourished in Delhi and later in Avadh, a state covering an area around the city of Lucknow. Avadh does not exist as a state now, and the area is presently part of the state of Uttar Pradesh.

The Moghlai cuisine is characterized by use of dairy products (cream, yogurt, paneer cheese, sour cream and milk), dry fruits and nuts (cashews, almonds, pistachios, pine nuts, raisins), as well as some fresh fruits (sometimes fresh grapes and orange juice), and exotic spices (black cumin, cardamom, cinnamon, cloves, mace, nutmeg and saffron). Rose or kewda water are used sometimes to impart a flowery perfumed scent to the dishes. In India, no other cuisine is as popular as Moghlai. It has become an accepted standard for fine cuisine in upscale restaurants and is the food of choice for such special occasions as weddings and graduations.

Hara Bhara Kabob (Potato, Spinach and Pea Cakes)

On my visits to India during the past few years, I've noticed this appetizer on the menus of many reputable restaurants, but I haven't seen it elsewhere in the United States yet. At Ajanta, it appears on the menu as part of the monthly specials and is very popular.

INGREDIENTS (Serves 6)

2 slices white bread, crusts removed

1 cup spinach, coarsely chopped

1 cup frozen green peas, microwaved on high for 3 minutes

1/2 cup loosely packed cilantro, coarsely chopped

4 medium potatoes, boiled, peeled and mashed (about 1 1/2 cups mashed)

1 teaspoon salt

2 teaspoons ajwain seeds

1 green chile pepper, chopped

Oil for pan frying

1. Tear bread into 2-inch pieces, then drop into a food processor and grind into bread crumbs. Add spinach, peas and cilantro to the processor bowl and continue processing by pulsing until the ingredients are mixed. Do not overprocess; leave some texture in the mixture. Transfer to a bowl and mix in the remaining ingredients, except oil. Divide into twelve equal portions. Shape each portion into a round cake about 1/2 inch thick. It will be helpful to smear a bit of oil on your palms before making cakes.

2. Heat oil about 1/4 inch deep in a sauté pan. When very hot, almost to smoking point, place 3 or 4 cakes in the oil and fry until crisp and brown, about 2 minutes on each side. Repeat with the remaining cakes. Drain on a plate lined with paper towels. Frying too many cakes at one time will reduce the temperature of the oil and the cakes may fall apart and soak up too much oil. Serve warm with Mint Cilantro Chutney (see page 47).

Lamb Korma Shahjahani (Lamb in Creamy Curry Sauce)

This is a rather fancy version of lamb curry. Named after a Moghul emperor, this lamb dish has a rich, creamy sauce. Finished with a sprinkle of slivered almonds, this dish is worthy of royalty.

INGREDIENTS (Serves 6)

4 tablespoons oil

2 teaspoons cumin seeds

1-inch piece ginger, peeled and finely chopped

3 to 4 medium onions, peeled, quartered and thinly sliced

2 pounds boneless cubed lamb, defatted (weigh after boning and defatting)

1 1/2 teaspoons turmeric powder

2 teaspoons salt

2 teaspoons paprika

1/2 to 1 teaspoon hot chile pepper powder

1 teaspoon black pepper powder

3 teaspoons coriander powder

1 cup plain yogurt

2 teaspoons Garam Masala (see recipe on page 24)

1/2 cup heavy cream

1/2 cup slivered almonds

1. Heat oil in a 6-quart saucepot When hot, add cumin seeds (oil should be hot enough to sizzle when seeds are added; test by dropping a couple of seeds in first). When the seeds sizzle, add ginger. Fry for about 15 seconds.

2. Add onions and sauté over medium-high heat, stirring frequently, until the onions become slightly brown.

3. Raise to high heat. When the pot becomes very hot, add lamb. Stir and sauté until the lamb is nicely browned and most of the moisture has evaporated. Add turmeric, salt, paprika, chile pepper powder, black pepper powder and coriander powder. Stir for two to three minutes. Turn off the heat and add yogurt (the heat is turned off to prevent yogurt from curdling); mix. Turn the heat back on.

4. Bring the mixture to a boil. Add 1/4 to 1/2 cup of water if there is not enough liquid. Reduce heat, cover partially and simmer over low heat for 25 to 35 minutes, or until lamb becomes tender. At this point, there should be a thin film of oil on the top surface. Add Garam Masala and cream. Mix and cover, then turn off the heat and leave it on the stove for about 5 minutes. Sprinkle slivered almonds on top before serving.

Lamb Korma Shahjahani (Lamb in Creamy Curry Sauce)

Khumb Jahanara (Mushrooms with Creamed Spinach and Spices)

Named after a Moghul empress, this is yet another dish fit for royalty. Even if you do not like spinach, you will love this dish.

INGREDIENTS (Serves 6)

2 tablespoons oil

8 to 10 medium cloves garlic, chopped

1 green chile, chopped (optional)

1-inch piece ginger, scraped and chopped

2 medium onions, chopped

3 medium tomatoes, chopped

1 1/2 teaspoons salt, or to taste

2 teaspoons coriander powder

2 teaspoons cumin powder

1 teaspoon turmeric

1 teaspoon paprika

1/2 to 2 teaspoons hot chile pepper powder, to taste

4 cups fresh spinach, chopped

3 tablespoons chickpea flour

3/4 pound shiitake mushrooms, stems removed, cut in 1/4-inch slices

1/2 cup whipping cream

1/2 cup ground cashews

1. Heat the oil in a 6- to 8-quart saucepot. When hot, add garlic, green chile and ginger. Sauté for about 30 seconds. Add onions and sauté over medium-high to high heat for 10 to 12 minutes, or until translucent. Add chopped tomatoes, salt and all the spices. Cook for about 5 minutes.

2. Add chopped spinach; stir and cook until all the spinach is wilted, about 5 minutes. Reduce to medium heat, partially cover and cook for 5 minutes. Transfer to a food processor and grind the mixture. Transfer back to the pot.

3. Add chickpea flour, mixing thoroughly with a whisk to make sure the flour does not become lumpy. Add mushrooms. Partially cover and cook another 10 minutes. Add whipping cream and ground cashews. Mix thoroughly and then remove from heat.

Yakhani Pulav (Rice with Onions and Broth)

In this rice preparation, the rice picks up a beautiful golden color from the caramelized onions.

INGREDIENTS (Serves 6)

2 tablespoons oil

1 medium onion, cut in quarters and thinly sliced

2 cups basmati rice

4 cups chicken or lamb broth

1 1/2 teaspoons salt (or less if there is salt in the broth)

2 sticks cinnamon

2 to 3 bay leaves

1. Heat the oil in an 8-quart saucepot. Add onion and sauté until dark golden brown.

2. Add rice. Sauté for about 3 to 4 minutes or until opaque. Add broth, salt and remaining ingredients. Bring to a boil. Reduce to low heat, cover and cook until all the moisture is absorbed, about 20 to 25 minutes. Remove from stove and fluff the rice with a fork.

Ajwaini Naan (Leavened Dough Flat Bread Flavored with Ajwain)

This is a variation on the Naan bread recipe on page 78. Instead of ajwain seeds, or as a variation, you can substitute sesame or nigella seeds.

INGREDIENTS (Serves 6)

1 1/2 teaspoons dry activated yeast	3/4 to 1 cup water
2 tablespoons oil	Flour for dusting
1 egg	2 tablespoons ajwain seeds
1/2 teaspoon salt	Melted butter to brush on the cooked naan
1/2 cup plain yogurt	
4 cups loosely packed white flour	

1. In a large bowl, add yeast, oil, egg, salt and yogurt to the flour and mix thoroughly. Add water gradually, working it into the flour and kneading it into a soft, supple dough. Do not use all the water at once— add it gradually and use only enough to make a soft dough. The exact quantity of water will vary depending on the type of flour used and how accurately it was measured. Place in a nonreactive bowl large enough for the dough to rise. Cover and let the dough rise for about 4 to 6 hours.

2. Divide dough into eight equal parts. Make each part into a round ball and leave it on a tray or baking sheet, loosely covered with plastic wrap, to rise a second time for 3 to 4 hours.

3. Turn the oven to broil and let heat for about 15 minutes.

4. Pick up a ball of dough and dust it with the flour. With a rolling pin, roll dough balls into flat circles about 8 inches in diameter and 1/8 inch thick. Sprinkle about 1/2 teaspoon of ajwain seeds on the naan and pat the seeds so they become embedded in the dough. Place the flat, rolled-out bread on a baking sheet and set it under the broiler for 30 to 40 seconds, or until the top surface of the naan becomes light golden

brown. Remove the tray from the broiler, turn the naan and cook it on the other side for about 20 seconds. The second side should be just cooked, not golden brown.

5. Remove from the broiler and brush with melted butter. Repeat until all the naan are cooked. The bread should be cooked just before eating dinner, after the rest of the cooking is finished.

Ajwaini Naan (Leavened Dough Flat Bread Flavored with Ajwain)

Rasmalai (Paneer Cheese Cakes in Thickened Milk Sauce)

Whenever we have Indian guests at Ajanta, this is one dessert that they always order. The thickened milk sauce is absolutely delicious.

INGREDIENTS (Serves 6)

Thickened Milk Sauce:

1/2 gallon half-and-half

Seeds from 6 to 8 cardamom pods

1/2 cup sugar

2 tablespoons kewda water

Paneer Cakes:

1/2 gallon milk
1/2 cup vinegar

2 tablespoons white flour

1/4 teaspoon baking powder

3 cups water

2 cups sugar

1/4 cup chopped pistachios, for garnish

For Thickened Milk Sauce:

1. In a thick 6- to 8-quart saucepot, bring half-and-half to a boil over medium to high heat. Stir every minute or so with a wire whisk, scraping the bottom to dislodge any milk solids to prevent a burnt flavor. Add cardamom seeds during this time. Once it starts boiling, reduce heat to medium and continue to thicken the half-and-half, stirring every 5 minutes or so for the next 1 to 1 1/2 hours, or until the half-and-half is reduced to about a third of its original volume. Check the volume by dipping a wooden spoon or a ruler in the liquid and measuring the height before and after thickening.

2. Add sugar and stir to dissolve. Let cool. Add kewda water, and refrigerate.

For Paneer Cakes:

1. Bring milk to a boil, stirring often to prevent milk solids from sticking to the bottom of the pot. Turn off the heat when milk starts to boil. Let cool for about 10 minutes. Add vinegar in a steady stream and stir;

the milk will curdle. Let cool for another 20 minutes, and then pour into a colander lined with muslin cloth (the colander should be placed in a sink or tray to catch the whey). Lift up four corners of the muslin cloth, twist around the cheese and squeeze out the excess whey. Release the pressure and squeeze again three or four times. The whey will squeeze out in a stream first and then in drops. Do not over-squeeze; stop when whey starts to drip out in drops.

NOTE: This step is critical for the final results. Squeezing out the whey completely will make rasmalai hard. On the other hand, if less whey is squeezed out the rasmalai will fall apart when cooked in the syrup in step three. You might have to experiment to get it just right.

2. Transfer paneer cheese (called "chenna" at this stage) to a large bowl or tray. Add flour and baking powder and knead firmly with your palm to mash the granules. Divide the mixture into twelve portions, and form each portion into a patty or cake about 1 1/2 to 2 inches in diameter.

3. Boil water in an 8-quart saucepot. The pan should be large enough in its diameter to accommodate cakes for poaching in a single layer. Add sugar and stir to dissolve. Bring to a boil and cook rasmalai cakes in the boiling, foamy syrup over high heat for about 10 minutes. The cakes will acquire a sponge-like consistency. Remove from heat and let cool.

4. Bring out the thickened milk sauce from the refrigerator. Gently squeeze out excess syrup from the rasmalai cakes and add to the milk sauce. Garnish with chopped pistachios and serve.

Rasmalai (Paneer Cheese Cakes in Thickened Milk Sauce)

Moghlai Feast Shopping List

FROM YOUR REFRIGERATOR AND PANTRY

Ginger	2 inch piece
Garlic	8 cloves
Oil	
Sugar	2 1/2 cups
Whole milk	1/2 gallon
Almonds, slivered	1/2 cup
Cashews, ground	1/2 cup
Salt	
White bread	2 slices
All-purpose flour	5 cups
Dry activated yeast	1 1/2 teaspoons
Baking powder	1/4 teaspoon
Large egg	1
Butter	1/4 stick
Frozen green peas	1 cup
White vinegar	1/2 cup

FROM YOUR INDIAN SPICE RACK

Turmeric	2 1/2 teaspoons
Paprika	3 teaspoons
Coriander powder	2 teaspoons
Hot chile pepper powder	3 teaspoons
Cumin powder	2 teaspoons
Cumin seeds	2 teaspoons
Cardamoms	8 pods
Cinnamon sticks	2
Ajwain seeds	4 teaspoons
Black pepper powder	1 teaspoon
Bay leaves	3
Garam Masala	2 teaspoons
Kewda water	2 tablespoons

SUPERMARKET SHOPPING LIST

Red potatoes	4 medium
Onions	8 medium
Tomatoes	4 medium
Cilantro	2 1/2 cups
Mint	1 cup
Mushrooms (Shiitakes recommended)	3/4 pound
Green chile peppers	3
Spinach	5 cups
Plain yogurt	1 1/2 cups
Whipping cream	1 cup
Half-and-half	1/2 gallon
Chicken broth	4 cups
Lamb, boneless, cubed	2 pounds

SPECIALTY SHOPPING

Basmati rice	2 cups
Chickpea flour	3 tablespoons
Tamarind Concentrate	2 x 2-inch piece

Sufed Maas (Lamb in White Sauce)

Feast from Rajasthan

LOCATED IN THE WESTERN FRONTIER REGION of India bordering Pakistan, the state of Rajasthan covers most of the Thar Dessert. Its exotic palaces make Rajasthan the number-one tourist state in the country. The Rajasthani joy of life is exemplified in their colorful clothes and in the year-round excitement of festivals and fairs. I was born in the state of Sindh. When Sindh was converted to Pakistan, our family migrated to Rajasthan. I grew up in Rajasthan and lived there until I graduated from the University of Jodhpur. I have fond memories of its people and their culture.

Most Rajasthani food is quite similar to North Indian cuisine. Hot peppers are used liberally, reflecting the Rajasthani zest for life. Food eaten by royalty shows pronounced influence from Moghlai cuisine. Certain dishes, however, have evolved in Rajasthan and are not found elsewhere. The dishes featured here fall into this category.

Bharwan Mirch Pakora
(Stuffed Chile Pepper Fritters)

I vividly remember as a school kid buying stuffed chile pepper pakoras for a midday snack and thoroughly enjoying them. (See photo page 6.)

INGREDIENTS (Serves 6)

Stuffing:

2 medium potatoes, boiled

1/2 teaspoon salt

1 teaspoon dried pomegranate seeds, crushed or coarsely ground

1 teaspoon chile flakes

1/4 cup loosely packed chopped cilantro

3 large poblano or pasilla peppers

Batter:

1 cup loosely packed chickpea flour

1 teaspoon baking powder

1 teaspoon ajwain seeds

1/2 teaspoon salt

1/2 cup water

Oil for deep-frying

1. Peel and cut boiled potatoes into 1/4-inch dice. Mix with remaining ingredients except the peppers for the stuffing. Divide the stuffing into six equal parts. Set aside.

2. Cut each pepper into two halves by slicing along its length. Remove stem and seeds from each half, then fill with the stuffing. Set aside.

3. Prepare the batter by mixing together all the ingredients except the oil with a wire whisk until the batter is smooth and there are no lumps. If the batter does not stick to the peppers, mix in about 1 more tablespoon chickpea flour.

4. Heat the oil to about 325 to 350 degrees in a deep-fryer. Using a large spoon, dip stuffed peppers in the batter, and then deep-fry 3 peppers at a time at medium to medium-high heat until golden brown. Frying too many peppers at one time will reduce the temperature of the oil and the pakoras will soak up too much oil. Serve hot with Sweet-and-Sour Tamarind Chutney (see page 73).

Making Bharwan Mirch Pakora (Stuffed Chile Pepper Fritters)

Sufed Maas (Lamb in White Sauce)

The word sufed is Hindi for "white." All the ingredients used in the sauce for this dish are white, hence its name. This unusual dish has a delicious sauce that does not taste or look like a curry. The dish originates from the royal kitchens of Rajasthan.

INGREDIENTS (Serves 6)

3 tablespoons oil

1-inch piece ginger, peeled and finely chopped

3 medium onions, quartered and thinly sliced 1/16 inch thick

2 pounds boneless cubed lamb, defatted (weigh after boning and defatting)

1 1/2 teaspoons salt

2 teaspoons white poppy seeds

3 teaspoons cardamom powder

2 teaspoons white pepper powder

2 green chiles, or to taste, finely chopped

1/3 cup plain yogurt

1/2 cup coconut milk

1/3 cup blanched almonds, ground

1/3 cup heavy cream

2 tablespoons lemon juice

1. Heat the oil in a 6- to 8-quart saucepot. When hot, add ginger and sauté for 15 to 20 seconds.

2. Add onions and sauté over medium-high heat, stirring frequently, until the onions become soft.

3. Raise to high heat. When the pot becomes very hot, add lamb and sauté until it is nicely browned and most of the excess moisture has evaporated. Reduce heat to medium or medium-high and add salt, poppy seeds, cardamom, pepper and chiles. Stir-fry

for 2 to 3 minutes, and then add yogurt, coconut milk and almonds.

4. Bring the mixture to a boil (add 1/4 to 1/2 cup of water if there is not enough liquid), reduce heat and simmer, partially covered, over low heat for 30 to 45 minutes, or until lamb becomes tender. The sauce should have the consistency of buttermilk. If it is too thick, add 2 to 4 tablespoons water. If the sauce is too watery, cook with the lid off for a few minutes to thicken it. Mix in cream and lemon juice, cover, turn off the heat and leave it on the stove for about 5 minutes.

Achari Baingan (Stuffed Eggplant)

In this dish, long eggplants are stuffed with a spice mixture and then sautéed. The stuffing is made with spices generally used for making Indian pickles, which are known for their intense tart flavor. This dish has some of that quality. In Rajasthan, it is made very hot. Cook this dish as hot as your palate will permit. (See photo page 20.)

INGREDIENTS (Serves 6)

2 pounds Chinese or Japanese eggplants, 6 to 8 inches long

1 teaspoon salt

3 tablespoons oil

1 teaspoon black mustard seeds

1 teaspoon cumin seeds

1 teaspoon nigella seeds

1 teaspoon fenugreek seeds

1-inch piece ginger, chopped

8 medium cloves garlic, chopped

2 medium onions, chopped

4 medium tomatoes, chopped

1 1/2 teaspoons salt, or to taste

3 teaspoons coriander powder

1 1/2 teaspoons turmeric

1 1/2 teaspoons paprika

1/2 to 2 teaspoons crushed chile peppers

About 1/4 cup oil for sautéing

1. Remove stems from the eggplants and then cut them in half lengthwise, leaving them joined together at the stem end. Lightly salt the eggplants and leave them to drain in a colander for 30 minutes or more, while preparing the stuffing.

2. Heat 3 tablespoons oil in a 10-inch skillet. When hot, add mustard and cumin seeds. When the mustard seeds pop, add nigella seeds, fenugreek seeds, ginger and garlic. Fry for about 30 seconds and then add chopped onions. Sauté onions until soft, about 10 minutes. Add tomatoes, salt and the remaining spices; stir and cook, uncovered, for 20 minutes, or until the mixture becomes very thick and quite dry. The mixture will have a sheen from the oil when it is ready. (If the mixture is not dry enough, it will ooze out when stuffed into the eggplant.) Let cool.

3. Stuff a tablespoon of the mixture into each eggplant.

113

4. Heat 1/4 cup oil in a large skillet. Place eggplants in the oil in a single layer. Sauté over medium heat, turning eggplants with a pair of tongs every 3 to 4 minutes until the eggplants are cooked, for about 10 to 12 minutes (or longer). The cooking time will depend on the level of heat and size of the eggplants. Serve hot.

Making Achari Baingan (Stuffed Eggplant)

Rajasthani Pulav
(Rice with Spices)

INGREDIENTS (Serves 6)

2 tablespoons oil

1 medium onion, cut in quarters and thinly sliced

Seeds from 8 cardamom pods

10 whole cloves

10 peppercorns (optional)

2 (2-inch) cinnamon sticks

2 cups basmati rice

4 cups chicken or lamb broth or water

1 1/2 teaspoons salt (or less if there is salt in the broth)

1. In a 6- to 8-quart saucepot, heat the oil. Add onion and spices. Sauté until onion becomes golden brown.

2. Add rice and sauté, stirring, for about 3 minutes. Add broth or water and salt. Bring to a boil. Reduce to low heat, cover and cook for 15 to 20 minutes, or until all the moisture is absorbed. Remove from stove and fluff the rice with a fork.

Batia Roti (Rajasthani Salted Flat Bread)

A variation of Indian Chapati bread, distinguished by use of salt, cilantro and spices.

INGREDIENTS (Serves 6)

2 cups Chapati flour or other whole-wheat , low-gluten, pastry-grind flour

2 tablespoons oil

3/4 to 1 cup water

1 tablespoon salt

1 1/2 tablespoons cumin seeds, toasted and coarsely ground

1 tablespoon black peppercorn, coarsely ground

1/4 cup chopped cilantro

Flour for dusting

1/2 cup oil or melted butter for frying

1. Mix flour and 2 tablespoons oil. Add water gradually, working it into the flour, mixing and kneading. Do not use all the water at once; add it gradually and use only what is necessary. The exact quantity of water will vary depending on the type of flour used. Knead the dough well until it is supple and elastic. Cover the dough with a damp cloth and set aside for about 30 minutes.

2. In a separate bowl, mix salt, spices and cilantro and divide mixture into eight equal parts.

3. Heat a griddle on high heat. Turn the heat down to medium once the griddle is hot.

4. Divide the dough into eight portions. Form each portion into a small round ball. Flatten the balls, dust them with a little flour and, with a rolling pin, roll them out on a flat surface into circles about 5 inches in diameter. Spread one portion of the cilantro mixture evenly onto each rolled-out piece of dough. Roll the bread in a cylinder as shown, then roll the cylinder into a spiral. Press to flatten it, forming a disc. Roll out the flattened disc into a flat bread, about 9 inches in diameter.

5. Bake rolled-out bread on the griddle for about 30 to 40 seconds on each side. Smear the top side with oil and flip to fry for 15 to 20 seconds. Repeat on the other side. The finished bread should have golden brown spots.

Making Batia Roti (Rajasthani Salted Flat Bread)

Rasgulla (Paneer Cheese Balls in Syrup)

Indians love rasgullas. Whenever I serve it to my American friends, they say it is very good, but they do not seem to fall in love with it. It might be an acquired taste. I am including the recipe because the city of Bikaner, Rajasthan, where I spent my childhood, is famous for its rasgullas.

INGREDIENTS (Serves 6)

Paneer Cheese Balls:

1/2 gallon milk

1/2 cup vinegar

1 tablespoon white flour

2 teaspoons semolina (Cream of Wheat)

1/4 teaspoon baking powder

Syrup:

4 cups water

2 cups sugar

2 tablespoons kewda water

1. In a 6- to 8-quart saucepot, bring milk to a boil, stirring often to prevent milk solids from sticking to the bottom of the pot. Turn off the heat. Let cool for about 10 minutes. Add vinegar in a steady stream and stir. The milk will curdle. Let cool for another 20 minutes or so, and then pour milk and cheese in a colander lined with a damp muslin cloth (the colander should be placed in a sink). Lift up four corners of the muslin cloth, twist around the cheese and squeeze out the excess whey. Release the pressure and squeeze again three or four times. The whey will squeeze out in a stream first and then in drops. Do not over-squeeze; stop when whey starts to drip out in drops.

2. Transfer paneer cheese to a large bowl. Add flour, semolina and baking powder. Knead firmly with your palm to mash the granules. Divide the mixture into twelve portions and form each into a ball about 1 to 1 1/2 inches in diameter. Set aside.

3. Boil water in a 6- to 8-quart saucepot. Add sugar and stir to dissolve. Cook rasgulla balls in boiling, foamy syrup over medium to high heat for about 15 minutes. During the boiling process, slowly add about 1 tablespoon of water every 2 to 3 minutes. The balls will acquire a sponge-like consistency in about 15 minutes. Remove from heat and let cool. Add kewda water and refrigerate. Serve cold.

Rajasthan Feast Shopping List

FROM YOUR REFRIGERATOR AND PANTRY

Ginger	2 inch piece
Garlic	8 cloves
Oil	
Sugar	2 1/4 cups
Whole milk	1/2 gallon
White vinegar	1/2 cup
Almonds, blanched	1/3 cup
Salt	
All-purpose flour	1 tablespoon
Cream of wheat, regular	2 teaspoons
Baking powder	1 1/4 teaspoons
Butter	1/2 stick

FROM YOUR INDIAN SPICE RACK

Turmeric	1 1/2 teaspoons
Paprika	2 1/2 teaspoons
Coriander powder	3 teaspoons
Hot chile pepper powder	2 teaspoons
Crushed chile pepper /Chile flakes	2 teaspoons
Cardamom powder	3 teaspoons
White pepper powder	2 teaspoons
Cumin seeds	2 1/2 teaspoons
Black mustard seeds	1 teaspoon
White poppy seeds	2 teaspoons
Nigella seeds	1 teaspoon
Fenugreek seeds	1 teaspoon
Cardamoms	8 pods
Cinnamon sticks	2
Cloves	10 cloves
Ajwain seeds	1 teaspoon
Garam Masala	
Dried pomegranate seeds, crushed	1 teaspoon
Black peppercorns	2 tablespoon
Kewda water	2 tablespoons

SUPERMARKET SHOPPING LIST

Red potatoes	2 medium
Onions	6 medium
Tomatoes	4 medium
Cilantro	1 bunch
Green chile peppers	3
Large poblano or pasilla peppers	3
Lemons	1
Chinese eggplants, 6 to 8 inches long	2 pounds
Plain yogurt	1/3 cup
Whipping cream	1/3 cup
Chicken broth	4 cups
Lamb, boneless, defatted, cubed (weight after boning and removing fat)	2 pounds

SPECIALTY SHOPPING

Basmati rice	2 cups
Chickpea flour	1 cup
Chapati flour (Can substitute low-gluten, whole-wheat, pastry-grind flour)	2 cups
Coconut milk	1/2 cup
Tamarind Concentrate	2 x 2-inch piece

Machi Rai Masala (Catfish in Mustard Sauce)

Feast from Bengal

BENGAL, LOCATED IN EASTERN INDIA, north of the Bay of Bengal, was divided in 1947 when the British left India. East Bengal, with a majority population of Muslims, became East Pakistan and eventually Bangladesh, in 1971. West Bengal became a state of India. Bengalis are intellectuals, proud and passionate people. They refer to their state as Sonar Bangla, or "Golden Bengal." Bengalis are known for their art, literature and movies. Nobel laureate Rabindranath Tagore and filmmaker Satyajit Ray are two Bengalis who are famous worldwide.

Bengali passion extends to the cuisine, and Bengalis consider themselves the greatest lovers of food in the Indian subcontinent. Fish and seafood cooked in a variety of ways are an important part of Bengali cuisine. Freshwater fish is preferred, and Bengal's countless number of rivers, ponds and lakes are a source of several varieties. Hilsa, similar to American shad in taste and texture, is the most popular.

An abundance of water enables Bengalis to grow plenty of rice. Rice-based dishes and pilafs are consumed with almost every meal. Vegetables and coconut also grow abundantly and are included in day-to-day cooking. One of the distinctive flavors in Bengali cuisine comes from panchphoran, a mixture of five seed spices—cumin, fenugreek, black mustard, fennel and nigella. Aside from adding flavor, this seed mixture provides a textural contrast to the sauces.

Jhingri Pakora (Shrimp Fritters)

These are very addictive. I find it difficult to stop eating these every time I cook them.

INGREDIENTS (Serves 6)

1/2 cup chickpea flour

1/2 cup rice flour

1 cup large uncooked shrimp, peeled and deveined, cut in 1/2-inch pieces

1 teaspoon white poppy seeds

1 teaspoon ajwain seeds

1 teaspoon coriander seeds

1 teaspoon salt

1/2 teaspoon turmeric

1/2 teaspoon baking powder

1 teaspoon chile flakes

1/4 cup loosely packed chopped cilantro

Water

Oil for deep-frying

1. Mix all the ingredients except oil and add just enough water to make a thick paste.

2. Heat the oil in a wok to about 300 to 325 degrees. Using a large spoon, drop 5 to 6 large balls of the paste, about 1 to 2 inches in diameter, into the oil and deep-fry to golden brown over medium heat. This may take 6 to 8 minutes for each batch. Do not fry too many balls at one time. Oil may become cold and the balls may soak up too much oil. Remove fried balls and place on paper towels to drain. Repeat until the entire mixture is finished.

3. Serve warm with Mint Cilantro Chutney (see page 47).

Jhingri Pakora (Shrimp Fritters)

Machi Rai Ma∧ala (Catfi∧h in Mu∧tard Sauce)

I ate this dish in a restaurant in Bombay a few years ago and liked it a lot. When I came back to Berkeley, I developed the recipe from my memory of the way it tasted. I think I came pretty close. Whenever featured at Ajanta, it has been a hit.

INGREDIENTS (Serve∧ 6)

5 tablespoons oil, divided

2 teaspoons mustard seeds

2 teaspoons nigella seeds

8 to 10 cloves garlic, chopped

3 medium onions, cut in quarters and thinly sliced

4 medium tomatoes, chopped

2 teaspoons turmeric

2 teaspoons paprika

1/2 to 2 teaspoons hot chile pepper powder, to taste

2 teaspoons cumin powder

2 teaspoons cracked mustard seeds (pulsed in a spice or coffee grinder)

2 teaspoons salt

1/2 cup ground almonds

2 to 2 1/2 pounds catfish fillets, cut in 2- to 3-inch pieces

1. Heat 3 tablespoons of oil in a 6- to 8-quart saucepot. When hot, add mustard seeds and nigella seeds. When mustard seeds begin to pop, add garlic and sauté for about 15 seconds. Add onions and sauté over medium-high heat until soft, about 12 to 15 minutes. Add tomatoes and stir-fry for 6 to 8 minutes.

2. Add turmeric, paprika, chile pepper powder, cumin, cracked mustard seeds and salt. Sauté for about 3 to 4 minutes. Add ground almonds, reduce heat and cook until the oil separates from the mixture, about 8 to 10 minutes. The sauce at this time should be the consistency of porridge.

3. In a large skillet, heat the remaining 2 tablespoons of oil. When hot to the point of smoking, add fish and cook on each side for about 1 minute. Transfer with a slotted spoon to the sauce in the saucepan. Cook another 1 to 2 minutes, or until fish is cooked and flakes easily.

Sorsé Begun (Eggplant with Tomatoes and Mustard Seeds)

A tasty dish that is relatively easy to prepare. As a variation, you can add about 1 cup diced boiled potatoes in step 3.

INGREDIENTS (Serves 6)

1 1/2 tablespoons mustard seeds

2 tablespoons water

3 tablespoons oil

1-inch piece ginger, peeled and finely chopped

2 medium onions, chopped

2 medium tomatoes, chopped

1 teaspoon turmeric

1 teaspoon paprika

1 teaspoon hot chile pepper powder, or less to taste

2 teaspoons coriander powder

1 teaspoon salt

1 large globe eggplant, cut in 3/4-inch cubes

1/4 cup chopped cilantro

1. Soak mustard seeds in 2 tablespoons of water for 1 hour. Grind into a paste in a blender or a spice grinder. Set aside.

2. Heat the oil in a 4- to 6-quart saucepan. When hot, add ginger and sauté for about 20 seconds. Add onions and sauté over medium-high heat until onions become soft, about 8 to 10 minutes. Add mustard paste and sauté for about 1 minute. Add tomatoes, all of the spices and salt. Stir and cook for 6 to 8 minutes.

3. Add and mix eggplant. Cover and cook for 8 to 10 minutes. Remove the lid and stir every 2 to 3 minutes.

Stop cooking when eggplant becomes tender. Sprinkle cilantro on top. Serve hot.

Sorsé Begun (Eggplant with Tomatoes and Mustard Seeds)

125

Bengali Pulav (Rice Pilaf with Spices and Peanuts)

Once you've eaten some of the rice pilafs from India, it might become difficult to like plain rice. This dish will certainly make you crave flavored rice all the time.

INGREDIENTS (Serves 6)

2 tablespoons oil	4 to 5 bay leaves
2 tablespoons butter	3 two-inch sticks cinnamon
1/2 cup peanuts	2 cups basmati rice
1/4 cup raisins	4 cups water
1-inch piece of ginger, peeled and finely chopped	1 1/2 teaspoons salt, or to taste
	1/2 teaspoon turmeric
Seeds from 15 cardamom pods	1 tablespoon sugar

1. In a 6- to 8-quart saucepot, heat the oil and butter. When hot, add peanuts and sauté until they become light brown. Remove with a slotted spoon and set aside. Add raisins to the oil and butter mixture and sauté until they puff up. Remove with a slotted spoon and set aside.

2. In the same oil and butter mixture, add ginger, cardamom, bay leaves and cinnamon. Sauté for about 20 seconds.

3. Add rice. Sauté for about 3 minutes. Add water, salt, turmeric and sugar. Bring to a boil. Reduce to low heat, cover and cook for about 15 to 20 minutes, or until all the liquid has been absorbed. Remove from stove and fluff the rice with a fork.

4. Mix in peanuts and raisins.

Luchi (Deep-Fried White-Flour Puffy Bread)

Bengalis consider Luchi a refined, sophisticated form of Poori bread cooked all over India. Luchi is generally made with white flour, whereas Poori bread is always made with whole wheat flour. As in Poori bread, Luchi puffs up like a balloon and looks very exotic.

INGREDIENTS (Serves 6)

2 cups white flour	3/4 cup plus 2 tablespoons water
1/2 teaspoon salt	Oil for deep-frying
1 1/2 tablespoons oil	

1. Mix all the ingredients except water. Add water gradually, working it into the flour, mixing and kneading. Do not use all the water at once; add it gradually and use only the amount necessary. Knead the dough well until it is supple and elastic. The exact quantity of water used will vary depending on the type of flour used. Leave the dough covered with a damp cloth for about 30 minutes to 1 hour.

2. Heat oil for deep-frying in a wok. Lower to medium heat once the oil is hot.

3. Divide the dough in sixteen portions and form into a small balls by squeezing it between your palms. Flatten balls, dust with a little flour and use a rolling pin to roll balls into circles about 4 to 6 inches in diameter and 1/16 inch thick.

4. Deep-fry until golden brown, turning the luchi once to fry on both sides. Luchi should puff up like a balloon when fried. If this does not happen, the oil is not hot enough. Stop frying and turn up heat to increase oil temperature before frying more. Place fried Luchi on a platter lined with paper towels. Serve warm.

Gulab Jamun (Deep-Fried Milk-Powder Balls in Rose-Scented Syrup)

This dessert is cloyingly sweet! Indians love it. It is also my wife's favorite dessert.

INGREDIENTS (Serves 6)

1 cup powdered milk

3 1/2 tablespoons all-purpose flour

1/8 teaspoon baking soda

1/2 cup heavy whipping cream

2 cups sugar

2 cups water

Seeds from 10 cardamom pods

Oil for frying

2 tablespoons rose water

1. Mix powdered milk, flour and baking soda in a bowl. Be sure to measure baking soda very carefully as using too much will make the Gulab Jamun very soft. Add whipping cream gradually while kneading the mixture. Add only as much cream as needed to make a dough.

2. In a 6- to 8-quart saucepot, heat sugar and water together to make syrup. Add cardamom seeds and stir to mix sugar and water. Turn off the heat when the sugar is dissolved.

3. Heat oil to 250 degrees F over a smaller burner.

4. Divide the dough in sixteen portions and roll between your palms into a smooth ball about 1 inch in diameter. Fry the rolled balls a few at a time on a very low heat (the balls should slowly sizzle), until they become golden brown. Dunk the fried balls into the syrup and let them soak for 30 minutes or more. Let the Gulab Jamun and the syrup cool to room temperature, and then add rose water. Warm to about 100 to 110 degrees F before serving. Serve Gulab Jamuns in the syrup.

Gulab Jamun (Deep-Fried Milk-Powder Balls in Rose-Scented Syrup)

FROM YOUR REFRIGERATOR AND PANTRY

Ginger	2 inch piece
Garlic	8 to 10 cloves
Oil	
Sugar	2 1/4 cups
Raisins	1/4 cup
Almonds	1/2 cup
Peanuts	1/2 cup
Salt	
All-purpose flour	2 1/2 cups
Baking powder	1/2 teaspoon
Baking soda	1/8 teaspoon
Butter	1/4 stick

FROM YOUR INDIAN SPICE RACK

Turmeric	4 teaspoons
Paprika	3 teaspoons
Coriander powder	2 teaspoons
Cumin powder	2 teaspoons
Hot chile pepper powder	3 teaspoons
Crushed chile pepper /Chile flakes	1 teaspoon
Coriander seeds	1 teaspoon
Mustard seeds	9 teaspoons
Nigella seeds	2 teaspoons
White poppy seeds	1 teaspoon
Cardamoms	25 pods
Cinnamon sticks	3
Ajwain seeds	1 teaspoon
Bay leaves	5
Rose water	2 tablespoons

SUPERMARKET SHOPPING LIST

Onions	6 medium
Tomatoes	8 medium
Cilantro	2 bunches
Mint	1 bunch
Green chile peppers	1
Eggplant, round, large	1
Whipping cream	1/2
Large size shrimp	3/4 pound
Catfish fillets	2 1/2 pounds
Milk powder	1 cup

SPECIALTY SHOPPING

Basmati rice	2 cups
Chickpea flour	1/2 cup
Rice flour	1/2 cup
Tamarind Concentrate	2 x 2-inch piece

Shrikhand (Saffron Yogurt)

Feast from Maharashtra

THE STATE OF MAHARASHTRA IS LOCATED on the west coast of India, overlooking the Arabian Sea. The name of the state means "the Great State." It is an appropriate name, since it is the largest state in India in terms of area as well as population. Mumbai (better known as Bombay) is the capital of Maharashtra. Mumbai is known for its movie industry (nicknamed Bollywood) as well as for being a major financial and business center.

The cuisine of Maharashtra has its own distinctive flavors and ingredients. Rice grows abundantly in the region and is the staple food grain. Coconuts also grow abundantly. Grated coconut, coconut milk and coconut oil are used liberally in most dishes. Peanuts and cashews are used in many dishes. Kokum, a souring agent commonly used for flavoring, is unique to Maharashtra. Kokum is a deep purple berry with a pleasant, fruity, sour flavor.

Fish and seafood are a major part of Maharashtrian cuisine in the coastal region of Konkan. Among seafood, the most popular fish is Bombay duck, normally fried and crisp. Pomfret and mackerel are also quite popular. In addition to fish, dishes prepared with shrimp, crab, lobster, clams, mussels and scallops are common.

The interior region of Maharashtra has spicier food. Dishes from Vidarbha and Khandesh do not have as much coconut but use a lot of peanuts and chickpea flour. Kolahpur is famous for its chile-hot meat and vegetable curries, usually red in color due to copious quantities of chiles used in the sauce. The cuisine from Aurangabad is influenced by Moghuls, who ruled the region, and consists of meat dishes like biriyanis, pulav and kabobs.

The Maharashtrian feast will be hot, so brace yourself before you sit down to eat.

Scallop Tikki (Spicy Scallop Cakes)

As the name suggests, this is an exotic appetizer. It certainly is an impressive way to start an evening.

INGREDIENTS (Serves 6)

1/2 pound large sea scallops cut in 1/4-inch dice

2 to 3 medium red potatoes, boiled, peeled and mashed (about 1 1/2 cups mashed)

Two slices of white bread, crust removed, processed into bread crumbs in a food processor

1-inch piece ginger, peeled and finely diced

1/4 cup loosely packed chopped cilantro

1/2 teaspoon salt

1 teaspoon chile flakes

1 teaspoon turmeric

2 teaspoons cumin powder

1 green chile pepper, finely chopped

Oil for shallow frying

1. Mix together all the ingredients except oil. Divide into six equal portions and form into round patties about 1/2 to 3/4 inch thick.

2. Heat oil 1/4 inch deep in a skillet. Fry 2 to 3 cakes at a time until they are nicely browned, about 2 minutes on each side. Make sure that the oil is very hot, otherwise the cakes will fall apart and soak up too much oil. Drain on paper towels. Serve with Mint Cilantro Chutney (see page 47).

Kolhapuri Gosht (Lamb Curry from Kolhapur)

Kolhapuri dishes are eaten spicy hot—actually fiery hot. I love hot food, and whenever I go to Mumbai, I seek out Maharashtrian restaurants and order this dish or Kolhapuri vegetarian dishes, if I can find them.

INGREDIENTS (Serves 6)

3 tablespoons oil

1 1/2-inch piece of ginger, peeled and chopped

3 to 4 dry red chiles, broken into 1/4-inch pieces

3 medium onions, quartered and thinly sliced

2 pounds boneless lamb, defatted and cubed (weigh after defatting)

1 teaspoon whole peppercorns

1 teaspoon whole cloves

1 1/2 teaspoons turmeric

4 teaspoons hot chile pepper powder, or to taste (substitute paprika, partially or fully, to make the dish mild)

2 teaspoons coriander powder

1 1/2 teaspoons salt, or to taste

3 medium tomatoes, chopped coarsely and pureed

1 cup coconut milk

3 to 4 sprigs curry leaves (optional)

1. Heat 2 tablespoons oil in a 6-quart saucepot. When hot, add ginger and broken red chiles. Sauté for about 20 seconds.

2. Add onions and sauté over high heat for about 12 to 15 minutes, stirring occasionally, or until the onions become golden brown. Turn the heat down a little if onions start to stick to the bottom of the pot.

3. Raise to high heat. Add cubed lamb. Sauté the lamb, stirring frequently, until it becomes nicely browned and most of the moisture has evaporated. Reduce to medium heat and add all the spices and salt. Sauté for 3 to 4 minutes, then add pureed tomatoes and coconut milk. Bring to a boil, reduce heat and simmer, uncovered, over low heat for about 45 minutes, or until the lamb becomes tender. Add curry leaves during the last few minutes of cooking.

Bhendichi Bhaji
(Okra and Potatoes with Spices)

Okra is one of my favorite vegetables, but only if it is prepared in a way that does not end up slimy. Fresh okra is available only for a limited time during summer. If you are preparing this dinner when okra is not in season, you can substitute green beans for okra.

INGREDIENTS (Serves 6)

3 tablespoons oil

2 teaspoons mustard seeds

2 medium potatoes, peeled and cut in 1/2-inch dice

1 1/2 pounds okra, trimmed (remove inedible top part) and sliced 1/2 inch thick

1/4 teaspoon asafetida

1 teaspoon turmeric

3 teaspoons coriander powder

1 teaspoon cumin powder

2 teaspoons hot chile pepper powder, or to taste (substitute paprika, partially or fully, to make the dish mild)

1 1/2 teaspoons salt

1/4 cup chopped cilantro

1. Heat oil in a 12-inch sauté pan. When hot, add the mustard seeds (oil should be hot enough that seeds pop when added; test by dropping a couple of seeds in first).

2. When seeds stop popping (about 10 seconds), add potatoes. Stir and sauté over high heat for 5 to 7 minutes.

3. Add sliced okra. Stir and sauté over high heat for about 10 minutes.

4. Add spices and salt. Reduce heat to medium and sauté another 10 minutes, or until the okra and potatoes are cooked.

5. Sprinkle chopped cilantro on top.

Bhendichi Bhaji (Okra and Potatoes with Spices)

Masala Bhat (Rice with Goda Spice Mix)

INGREDIENTS (Serves 6)

Rice:

2 tablespoons oil

2 cinnamon sticks

1 teaspoon cloves

4 bay leaves

2 cups basmati rice

4 cups water

1 1/2 teaspoons salt

Maharashtrian Goda Spice Mix:

Mix together, toast and grind:

1/4 cup shredded coconut, toasted

2 teaspoons coriander seeds

1 teaspoon cumin seeds

1 dry red chile

1/4 cup cashew pieces, sautéed

1/4 cup chopped fresh cilantro

1. Heat the oil in a 6- to 8-quart saucepot. When hot, add cinnamon sticks, cloves and bay leaves, and sauté for 10 seconds.

2. Add rice and sauté for 3 to 4 minutes, or until rice starts to change color and becomes opaque. Add water and salt.

3. Bring to a boil, add the Goda Spice Mix, turn down heat, cover and simmer until all the liquid is absorbed, about 15 to 20 minutes, and the rice is cooked.

4. Fluff the rice with a fork and garnish with cashews and cilantro.

Masala Bhat (Rice with Goda Spice Mix)

Pooran Poli (Lentil-Stuffed Flat Bread)

INGREDIENTS (Serves 6)

Dough:

2 cups chapati flour or other whole-wheat , low-gluten, pastry-grind flour

2 tablespoons oil

1 teaspoon salt

1 cup water

Daal mixture:

1 cup tuvar daal, (substitute other lentils if tuvar daal is not available)

4 cups water

1/2 teaspoon salt

1 teaspoon cardamom powder

5 cloves

2 teaspoons sugar

Flour for dusting

1/2 cup oil or ghee for griddle-frying

1. For the dough, mix flour, 2 tablespoons oil and salt. Add water gradually, working it into the flour, mixing and kneading. Do not use all the water at once; add it gradually and only use what is necessary. Knead the dough well until it is supple and elastic. Cover the dough with a damp towel and set aside for at least 30 minutes.

2. Place daal in a small saucepan, add about 4 cups water, salt and spices, cover, and then bring to a boil. Reduce heat and boil slowly until daal becomes soft, about 20 to 30 minutes. Make sure there is some water in the pan at all times, adding more water if necessary. When lentils become soft, drain the excess moisture. Transfer to a bowl, mix in sugar, and then mash the mixture with a potato masher.

3. Heat a griddle on high heat. Turn the heat down to medium heat once the griddle is hot.

4. Knead the dough again for 1 or 2 minutes and divide the dough into eight portions. Form each portion into small balls. Flatten the balls, dust them with a little flour and roll them out on a flat surface into circles about

5 inches in diameter. Put about 1 heaping tablespoon of daal mixture in the middle of the circle, close the dough around the mixture, seal it tight, dust it with flour, and re-roll the dough containing daal mixture into a circle about 7 to 8 inches in diameter.

5. Cook rolled-out bread on the griddle for about 30 to 40 seconds on each side. Smear the top side with oil and flip to fry for 15 to 20 seconds. Repeat on the other side. The cooked bread should have golden-brown spots.

Making Pooran Poli (Lentil-Stuffed Flat Bread)

Shrikhand (Saffron Yogurt)

(Photo on page 130)

INGREDIENTS (Serves 6)

4 cups plain yogurt (made from whole milk)

3/4 cup sugar

1 teaspoon cardamom powder

1/2 teaspoon saffron dissolved in 3 tablespoons warm milk

1/4 cup chopped pistachios, for garnish

2 tablespoons sunflower seeds, for garnish

1. Line a colander with a damp muslin cloth and pour yogurt in it. Place colander in a sink or on a tray to catch the whey that will drip from the colander. Cover and leave yogurt to drip for about 8 hours. Alternately, you can place yogurt in muslin cloth and tie it on the faucet so the whey drips directly into the sink.

2. Transfer thickened yogurt left in the muslin cloth to a 6- to 8-quart bowl. Add sugar, cardamom and saffron mixture. Whisk with a wire whisk for 7 to 8 minutes, or until the sugar dissolves and the yogurt becomes a smooth paste. Cover and chill in the refrigerator for at least 30 minutes.

3. Serve in ramekins or cups. Garnish with pistachios and sunflower seeds.

Making thickened yogurt

Maharashtra Feast Shopping List

FROM YOUR REFRIGERATOR AND PANTRY

Ginger	2 1/2 inch piece
Oil	
Sugar	1 cups
Cashew pieces	1/4 cup
Pistachios	1/4 cup
Sunflower seeds	1/8 cup
Salt	
White bread	2 slices
All-purpose flour	1/2 cup

FROM YOUR INDIAN SPICE RACK

Turmeric	2 1/2 teaspoons
Coriander powder	5 teaspoons
Cumin powder	3 teaspoons
Hot chile pepper powder	6 teaspoons
Asafetida	1/4 teaspoon
Crushed chile pepper /chile flakes	1 teaspoon
Cardamom powder	2 teaspoon
Dry red chiles	5
Peppercorns	1 teaspoon
Mustard seeds	2 teaspoons
Coriander seeds	2 teaspoons
Cumin seeds	1 teaspoon
Cinnamon sticks	2
Cloves	3 teaspoons
Saffron	1/2 teaspoon
Bay leaves	4

SUPERMARKET SHOPPING LIST

Red potatoes	5 medium
Onions	4 medium
Tomatoes	5 medium
Cilantro	2 bunches
Okra	1 1/2 pounds
Mint	1/2 bunch
Green chile peppers	2
Plain yogurt	4 cups
Whipping cream	
Large sea scallops	1/2 pound
Boneless lamb (weight after deboning and defatting)	2 pounds

SPECIALTY SHOPPING

Basmati rice	2 cups
Chapati flour (Can substitute low-gluten, whole-wheat, pastry-grind flour)	2 cups
Tamarind Concentrate	2 x 2-inch piece
Coconut milk	1 cup
Curry leaves (optional)	3 to 4 sprigs
Shredded coconut	1/4 cup
Tuvar daal	1 cup

Goanese Green Pulav (Rice and Vegetable Pilaf)

Feast from Goa

GOA IS A COASTAL STATE located about six hundred miles south of Bombay. Portugal ruled Goa from the sixteenth to mid-twentieth centuries. Prior to Portuguese rule, Goa was ruled by Muslims. The Portuguese rulers were responsible for one of the most brutal and wholesale religious conversions recorded in Asia. The result is a larger concentration of Christians in Goa—about 50 percent of the population—than anywhere else in India.

The cuisine of Goa is an intriguing combination of several influences. Goa is in South India, and South Indian influence is shown by the use of coconut and whole spices that are toasted or sautéed first and then ground up with some water to make an aromatic paste, which then becomes a base for the spicy sauce. The food in Goa is chile-hot, as in neighboring southern states. Being a coastal state, seafood is abundant and is a major part of Goanese cuisine.

Portuguese rule also left its mark on Goanese cooking. The Goanese prefer to eat meat, whereas the neighboring South Indians eat mostly vegetarian fare. Goanese Christians also eat pork and duck, meats that are generally not eaten in other parts of India. The use of vinegar as a souring agent is also distinctly Portuguese. The result of these influences is a cuisine that is distinctly pungent, piquant and hot.

Salmon Tikki (Salmon Cakes)

This recipe uses raw salmon rather than the cooked fish used in most fishcake recipes from India. The fish being cooked only once—in the cake form—stays moist and tastes much better than in recipes where the cakes use cooked fish.

INGREDIENTS (Serves 6)

1/2 pound boneless salmon fillet, skin off, cut into 1/4-inch dice

2 to 3 medium red potatoes, boiled, peeled and mashed (about 1 1/2 cups mashed)

2 slices white bread, crust removed, processed into bread crumbs

1-inch piece ginger, peeled and finely diced

2 teaspoons ajwain seeds

1/2 cup loosely packed chopped cilantro

1 1/2 teaspoons salt

1 teaspoon chile flakes

1 green chile pepper (serrano or jalapeño), finely chopped

Oil for pan frying

1. Thoroughly mix all the ingredients in a bowl. Divide into eight portions and form into cakes or patties.

2. Heat oil 1/4 inch deep in a skillet for pan frying. When hot, fry 2 to 3 salmon cakes at a time until golden brown, about 2 minutes on each side. Frying too many cakes at one time will reduce the temperature of the oil and the cakes will fall apart and soak up too much oil. Serve with Mint Cilantro Chutney (see page 47).

Galina Shakooti (Chicken with Coconut Milk and Spices)

I like the unusual combination of spices used in this dish. The sauce looks and tastes very different from the curry flavor and color normally associated with Indian cooking. It is a delicious sauce and the freshly sautéed and ground spices give off a wonderful aroma.

INGREDIENTS (Serves 6)

4 tablespoons vegetable oil, divided

1 1/2 teaspoons mustard seeds

3 to 10 dried, hot red chiles, broken into pieces

4 teaspoons white poppy seeds

1 1/2 teaspoons ajwain

1 1/2 teaspoons fenugreek seeds

3 teaspoons coriander seeds

6 to 8 cardamom pods

1/2 cinnamon stick

6 to 8 whole cloves

3 medium onions, quartered and sliced very thin, divided

2 pounds deboned and skinned chicken dark meat, cut into 1- to 2-inch pieces

1 1/2 teaspoons salt, or to taste

1 1/2 cups coconut milk

1 teaspoon black peppercorns

2 medium tomatoes, pureed

2 tablespoons lemon juice

1. In a 6- to 8-quart saucepot, heat 2 tablespoons oil. Oil should be so hot that the mustard seeds sizzle and pop when added. Add mustard seeds and sauté for about 10 to 15 seconds. When mustard seeds stop popping, add red chiles. After another 10 seconds, add poppy seeds, ajwain, fenugreek seeds, coriander seeds, cardamom pods, cinnamon stick and cloves. Fry for about 20 seconds and then add a fifth of the sliced onions. Sauté onions 6 minutes, or until soft. Transfer to a blender and puree the mixture to a thick paste, adding some water as necessary. Be sure the spices are ground fine in the paste.

2. Heat the remaining oil and sauté the remaining onions over medium-

high heat until slightly brown, about 8 to 10 minutes. Raise to high heat; wait 1 to 2 minutes until the pot gets hot. Add chicken pieces and stir-fry until they are browned and most of the moisture has evaporated.

3. Reduce to medium heat; add the spice-and-onion paste and salt. Stir for about 3 to 4 minutes, then add coconut milk, peppercorns and pureed tomatoes. Bring the mixture to a boil (add about 1/4 cup of water if there is not enough liquid). Reduce heat, cover and simmer slowly for about 20 to 25 minutes, or until chicken is tender. Stir in the lemon juice.

Galina Shakooti (Chicken with Coconut Milk and Spices)

Goanese Green Pulav (Rice and Vegetable Pilaf)

I often eat this one-pot dish with some yogurt on the side, which makes it a complete and balanced meal that is also very light and tasty. In this feast, it replaces separate rice and vegetable dishes (photo on page 142).

INGREDIENTS (Serves 6)

2 tablespoons oil

2 teaspoons caraway seeds

1 large onion, cut in half and sliced thinly

1 pound green beans, trimmed (cut 1/8 inch from each end) and cut in 1- to 2-inch pieces

1/2 cup fresh or frozen peas

1 1/2 cups basmati rice

2 cups water

1 teaspoon turmeric

2 to 3 sticks cinnamon

6 bay leaves

1 cup coconut milk

1 1/2 teaspoons salt

1 teaspoon whole peppercorns

1/2 cup roasted cashew pieces (roast in a skillet ahead of time with 1 teaspoon oil until golden brown)

1. Heat oil in a 6- to 8-quart saucepot. When oil is hot, fry caraway seeds for 10 seconds (the seeds should sizzle when added). Add onion and sauté until golden brown. Add green beans and peas (if using fresh peas; if using frozen peas, see step 3). Sauté for about 5 minutes.

2. Add rice and stir-fry over high heat for 4 to 5 minutes. Add water, turmeric, cinnamon sticks, bay leaves, coconut milk, salt and peppercorns.

3. Bring to a boil, reduce heat, cover and simmer for about 20 to 25 minutes, or until all the liquid is absorbed (add peas if using frozen peas). Cover and leave over very low heat for about 5 minutes. Remove from the stove, fluff up with a fork and mix in cashew pieces.

Goanese Poori (Deep-Fried Puffy Bread)

Poori is deep-fried bread that puffs up like a balloon during the process of frying. Popular all over India for special occasions, this bread has several regional differences. Goanese Poori uses a small amount of Cream of Wheat in the dough. Cream of Wheat makes poori stay puffed up longer, so it does not collapse quickly after being removed from the hot oil.

INGREDIENTS (Serves 6)

2 cups chapati flour or other low-gluten, whole-wheat, pastry-grind flour

1/2 teaspoon salt

1/2 cup Cream of Wheat

2 tablespoons oil

1 teaspoon sugar

3/4 to 1 cup water

Oil for deep-frying

Flour for dusting

1. Mix all the ingredients except water in a large, 4- to 6-quart bowl. Add water gradually, working it into the flour, mixing and kneading. Do not use all the water at once; add it gradually and use only what is necessary. Knead the dough well until it is supple and elastic. The exact quantity of water will vary depending on the type of flour used. Leave the dough covered with a damp cloth for about 30 minutes to 1 hour.

2. Heat oil for deep-frying in a wok or frying pan. Lower to medium heat once the oil is hot.

3. Divide the dough in sixteen portions and form small balls by rolling between your palms. Flatten balls, dust with a little flour and use a rolling pin to roll them into circles about 4 to 5 inches in diameter and 1/16 inch thick. It works well to roll each poori while the previous one is frying. Poories rolled-out ahead of time become sticky.

4. Fry poories about 15 seconds on each side, or until golden brown, turning them once. Place on a platter lined with paper towels. Serve warm.

Mango Mousse

This unusual dessert is one of the most popular at Ajanta. It can be made few hours ahead of time.

Iɴɢʀᴇᴅɪᴇɴᴛs (Sᴇʀᴠᴇs 6)

1 cup mango pulp (can use canned Alphonso mango pulp from India)

1 teaspoon cardamom powder

1 tablespoon lemon juice

2 tablespoons sugar (less if the mango is very sweet)

1 cup heavy cream

2 egg whites

1 1/2 packets (1/4 ounce each) unflavored gelatin powder

1/4 cup warm water

1. Mix together mango pulp, cardamom powder, lemon juice and sugar in a blender. Puree the mixture and leave in the blender.

2. Whip cream and egg whites in two separate bowls to soft peaks.

3. Dissolve gelatin in 1/4 cup of warm water. Make sure the gelatin is dissolved properly and has no lumps. Immediately add to the pureed mango pulp in the blender and mix thoroughly. If the gelatin is not mixed immediately, it will become granular and lumpy.

4. In a large bowl, fold together whipped cream, egg whites and mango mixture. Ladle into six small serving bowls. Refrigerate until the mixture is set, about 2 to 3 hours. Serve in the bowl or unmolded into a small dish.

Mango Mousse

FROM YOUR REFRIGERATOR AND PANTRY

Ginger	1 inch piece
Oil	
Sugar	3 tablespoons
Cashew pieces	1/2 cup
Salt	
White bread	2 slices
Frozen peas	1/2 cup
Cream of wheat, regular	1/2 cup
Eggs, large	2
Unflavored gelatin powder	2 packets (1/4 ounce each)

FROM YOUR INDIAN SPICE RACK

Turmeric	1 teaspoon
Cardamom powder	1 teaspoon
Crushed chile pepper /Chile flakes	1 teaspoon
Black peppercorns	2 teaspoons
Caraway seeds	2 teaspoons
Coriander seeds	3 teaspoons
Black mustard seeds	1 1/2 teaspoons
Cardamoms	8 pods
Cinnamon sticks	4
Cloves	8
Dried red hot chiles	3 to 10 (to taste)
Ajwain seeds	3 1/2 teaspoons
White poppy seeds	4 teaspoons
Fenugreek seeds	1 1/2 teaspoons
Bay leaves	6

SUPERMARKET SHOPPING LIST

Red potatoes	3 medium
Onions	6 medium
Tomatoes	3 medium
Cilantro	2 bunches
Mint	1/2 bunch
Green chile peppers	2
Lemons	2
Green beans	1 pound
Whipping cream	1 cup
Chicken	7 whole legs, boned and skinned
Boneless salmon fillet	1/2 pound
Mangoes	2 (to make 1 cup mango pulp)

SPECIALTY SHOPPING

Basmati rice	1 1/2 cups
Chapati flour (Can use low-gluten, whole-wheat, pastry-grind flour)	1 1/2 cup
Coconut milk	2 1/2 cups
Tamarind Concentrate	2 x 2-inch piece

151

Suji Halva (Cream of Wheat Pudding with Pistachios)

Feast from Hyderabad

HYDERABAD IS THE CAPITAL of the state of Andhra Pradesh, South India. The state of Andhra Pradesh is located on the east coast of south India, just north of Tamil Nadu (Madras). Hyderabad existed as a state until 1948, with Hyderabad city as its capital. The state of Hyderabad was one of the largest semi-autonomous kingdoms within India, ruled by Muslim rulers known as Nizaam. Soon after India became independent, Nizaam was persuaded into merging with the new democratic country, which surrounded it on all sides. A new state, Andhra Pradesh was formed, with Hyderabad as its capital.

Just as Moghlai cuisine evolved in north India as a marriage between North Indian and Muslim cuisine, Hyderabadi cuisine emerged in South India as a combination of South Indian and Muslim food. The end result is a cuisine that is rich with cream, milk, yogurt, nuts and fruits, and is highly aromatic with mustard seeds, cinnamon, cardamom, curry leaves, fennel and chile peppers. Coconut and tamarind are also used to flavor the dishes.

Masala Vadai (Spicy Lentil Cakes with Coconut Chutney)

INGREDIENTS (Serves 6)

1/2 cup toor daal*

1/2 cup urid daal*

1/2 cup chana daal*

4 1/2 cups water

2 green serrano or jalapeño chiles, finely chopped

1 medium onion, peeled and finely chopped

1 cup loosely packed chopped cilantro

1 to 1 1/2 teaspoons salt

2-inch piece ginger, chopped

Oil for pan frying

*see "daal" in chapter 2, "Indian Ingredients and Spices"

1. Pick over all daals to remove any foreign materials. Rinse two to three times. Soak daals in water for about 2 hours. Drain off excess water completely by pouring daals and water in a colander. Place in a food processor and grind to a coarse paste.

2. Add the remaining ingredients and mix thoroughly. Divide into twelve equal parts and form into cakes about 2 to 3 inches in diameter and 1/2 inch thick.

3. Heat oil, 1/4 inch to 1/2 inch deep, in a thick skillet. When hot almost to the smoking point, pan fry the lentil cakes until crisp and golden brown on both sides. Fry 3 to 4 cakes at a time. Frying too many cakes at one time will reduce the temperature of the oil and the cakes will fall apart and soak up too much oil. Serve with Coconut Chutney (recipe follows on page 155).

Coconut Chutney

About 3 to 4 tablespoons oil for pan frying

1/4 cup urid daal

1/2 cup shredded unsweetened coconut

2 green chiles, coarsely chopped

1 cup loosely packed chopped cilantro

1/2-inch piece ginger, peeled and chopped

1 teaspoon salt

3 tablespoons tamarind paste**

1 tablespoon oil

1 teaspoon cumin seeds

1 teaspoon mustard seeds

6 to 8 curry leaves (optional)

1/2 teaspoon asafetida (optional)

1. Heat oil for pan frying. Fry urid daal for a 2 to 3 minutes, or until it becomes golden brown. Drain on a paper towel. Put fried urid daal, coconut, green chiles, cilantro, ginger, salt and tamarind paste in a blender. Puree the ingredients, adding just enough water to do the blending. Transfer to a bowl.

2. In a small saucepan, heat 1 tablespoon oil. When very hot, add the last four ingredients and stir-fry for about 15 to 20 seconds. Remove from heat, add to the chutney paste and mix thoroughly. Taste and adjust for salt and sourness. Makes about 1 cup.

**To make tamarind paste, soak a lemon-size ball of tamarind for 1 hour in a small bowl with enough water to cover it. Mash with fingers to dissolve; strain and discard the solids. The final concentrate should be the consistency of thick buttermilk.

Hyderabadi Murg Korma (A Chicken Curry from Hyderabad)

This elegant chicken dish has a delicious sauce with a multitude of flavors and ingredients that are distinctively Hyderabadi.

INGREDIENTS (Serves 6)

3 tablespoons oil

8 to 10 cloves garlic, chopped

2-inch piece ginger, chopped

2 or 3 dried red chiles, broken into pieces

2 medium onions, quartered and thinly sliced

2 pounds deboned and skinned chicken dark meat, cut into 1 1/2- to 2-inch pieces

3 teaspoons cumin powder

1 1/2 teaspoons turmeric powder

1/2 to 2 teaspoons hot chile pepper powder, or to taste

2 teaspoons paprika

1 1/2 teaspoons salt, or to taste

1 cup coconut milk

1/2 cup ground cashews

1 cup yogurt

8 to 10 curry leaves

1 1/2 teaspoons Garam Masala (see page 24)

3 tablespoons lemon juice

1. Heat oil in a 6-quart saucepot. When hot, add garlic, ginger and chiles, and fry for about 15 seconds. Add onions and sauté over medium to high heat until slightly brown, about 10 to 12 minutes.

2. Raise to high heat, add chicken and stir-fry until browned, about 4 to 5 minutes. Continue browning until most of the moisture has evaporated.

3. Reduce to medium-high heat and add all the spices and salt. Stir for about 3 to 4 minutes; then add coconut milk, cashews and yogurt. Bring the mixture to a boil; add 4 to 6 tablespoons of water if there is not enough liquid. Reduce heat, cover and simmer slowly for about 20 to 25 minutes, or until chicken is tender. Add curry leaves, Garam Masala and lemon juice during the last 5 minutes of cooking.

Baghare Baingan (Eggplants Stuffed with Spice Paste)

This dish is made by sautéing eggplants stuffed with a mixture of cooked onions, spices, cashews and coconut. Stuffed eggplants are cooked throughout India. Among the many that I have tasted, this version is one of the best.

INGREDIENTS (Serves 6)

8 or 9 Chinese, Japanese or other long eggplants (6 to 8 inches long and about 1 1/2 inches in diameter)

2 to 3 teaspoons salt

6 tablespoons oil, divided

2 teaspoons cumin seeds

1 1/2 teaspoons fenugreek seeds

2-inch piece ginger, peeled and chopped

8 to 10 cloves garlic, chopped

3 medium onions, finely chopped

2 teaspoons turmeric

1/2 to 2 teaspoons hot chile pepper powder, or to taste (substitute all or part with paprika to make the dish mild)

3 teaspoons coriander powder

3 teaspoons white poppy seeds

3 teaspoons sesame seeds

2 teaspoons salt

1/4 cup thick tamarind paste, made by dissolving tamarind in warm water (directions on page 155)

3 tablespoons coconut powder

1/2 cup ground cashews

1. Remove stems from the eggplants. Make one lengthwise cut in each eggplant, but leave the two halves joined at the stem end. Sprinkle a pinch of salt in each eggplant and let drain for about 1 hour in a colander.

2. Meanwhile, heat 3 tablespoons oil in a sauté pan. When hot, add cumin and fenugreek seeds. Sauté for 10 to 15 seconds and then add the ginger and garlic. Sauté another 10 to 15 seconds and then add onions. Sauté onions for about 10 to 12 minutes over medium-high heat, or until onions are slightly browned. Add the spices and salt, and cook for 3 to 4 minutes. Add the remaining ingredients and continue cooking until the mixture almost dries out and is like a thick paste (the paste should have a sheen of oil released when the onions get cooked).

3. Dry eggplants with paper towels. Stuff about 1 1/2 to 2 tablespoons paste into each eggplant. In a large skillet, heat the remaining oil. Sauté the stuffed eggplants over medium to medium-high heat, turning once every 2 to 3 minutes until the eggplants are cooked, about 12 to 15 minutes. Use a pair of tongs to hold the eggplants by the stem end for turning. Check for doneness by inserting a fork; it should go in with slight resistance.

✦ Rice Dish ✦

Coconut Rice (Rice with Coconut and Spices)

INGREDIENTS (Serves 6)

1 1/2 tablespoons oil

2 teaspoons mustard seeds

2 cups basmati rice

3 cups water

1 teaspoon turmeric

1 cup coconut milk

1 1/2 teaspoons salt

Curry leaves from 2 sprigs

1 or 2 green chile peppers, chopped

1/2 cup cashew pieces

1. Heat the oil in a 6- to 8-quart saucepot. When hot, add mustard seeds and fry for about 10 seconds (oil should be hot enough to sizzle when seeds are added; test by dropping a couple of seeds in first). The mustard seeds will get toasted and start to pop.

2. Add rice and stir-fry over high heat for 2 to 3 minutes. Add water, turmeric, coconut milk, salt, curry leaves and chile peppers.

3. Bring to a boil, reduce heat, simmer and cook for about 20 to 25 minutes, or until all the liquid has been absorbed. Remove from the stove and mix in cashew pieces. Fluff the rice with a fork.

Raughani Roti (Whole Wheat Flat Bread)

This bread is like chapati bread on page 92, only much richer, since it has cream, butter and milk in the dough.

INGREDIENTS (Serves 6)

2 cups chapati or other low-gluten, whole-wheat, pastry-grind flour

3 tablespoons melted butter

4 tablespoons cream

1 teaspoon sugar

1 teaspoon salt

1/2 cup milk

Flour for dusting

Melted butter for brushing on the cooked roti

1. In a large bowl, mix flour, butter, cream, sugar and salt until the flour becomes crumbly. Add milk gradually, working it into the flour, mixing and kneading. Do not use all the milk at once; add it gradually and use only what is necessary. Knead the dough well until it is supple and elastic. The exact quantity of milk will vary depending on the type of flour used. Store in a bowl covered with a damp cloth for about 30 minutes to 1 hour.

2. Heat a griddle on high. Turn the heat down to medium once the griddle is hot.

3. Divide the dough into ten portions. Form each portion into a small ball. Flatten the balls, dust them with a little flour and roll them out into circles less than 1/8 inch thick.

4. Bake rolled-out roti on the griddle for about 30 to 40 seconds on each side. The cooked roti should have golden-brown spots. Remove from griddle, brush melted butter on tops and set aside. Repeat the process until all the roti are cooked. Roti should be cooked just before you sit down to eat, so they stay warm during the dinner.

Suji Halva (Cream of Wheat Pudding with Pistachios)

Whenever I have served this dish to my guests at home, they all have been very surprised that Cream of Wheat could taste so good. This dessert is fast and easy to prepare. At my dinner parties at home, I cook this dessert after the dinner is over and then serve it right away, as it is best eaten warm.

INGREDIENTS (Serves 6)

Pinch saffron

2 tablespoons hot water

1/2 cup (1 stick) butter

3 tablespoons slivered almonds

3/4 cup regular Cream of Wheat

1/2 cup sugar

1/2 cup milk

Seeds from 4 to 5 cardamom pods, crushed

3 tablespoons crushed pistachios

1. In a small bowl or cup, steep saffron in 2 tablespoons hot water.

2. Heat butter in a large skillet. Add almonds and stir until slightly brown. Add Cream of Wheat and cook for about 5 to 6 minutes over medium heat, stirring frequently. The Cream of Wheat will turn slightly brown.

3. Add remaining ingredients except pistachios. Cook for a 3 to 4 minutes over medium heat, stirring almost constantly, until the moisture has been absorbed and the Halva seems to bind together. Stir in saffron water. Turn off heat, transfer to a serving platter and garnish with pistachios. Serve warm.

Hyderabad Feast Shopping List

FROM YOUR REFRIGERATOR AND PANTRY

Ginger	4 (2- to 3-inch) pieces
Garlic	20 cloves
Oil	
Sugar	1/2 cup +1 tablespoon
Whole milk	1 cup
Almonds, slivered	3 tablespoons
Pistachios	3 tablespoons
Cashews	1 1/2 cups
Salt	
Cream of Wheat, regular	3/4 cup
Butter	1/2 +1 stick

FROM YOUR INDIAN SPICE RACK

Turmeric	5 teaspoons
Paprika	2 teaspoons
Coriander powder	3 teaspoons
Cumin powder	3 teaspoons
Hot chile pepper powder	4 teaspoons
Dried red chile	3
Cumin seeds	3 teaspoons
Black mustard seeds	3 teaspoons
Fenugreek seeds	1 1/2 teaspoons
White poppy seeds	3 teaspoons
Cardamoms	5 pods
Saffron	1/2 teaspoon
Sesame seeds	3 teaspoons
Garam Masala	1 1/2 teaspoons
Asafetida	1/2 teaspoon

SUPERMARKET SHOPPING LIST

Onions	6 medium
Cilantro	1 bunch
Green chile peppers	6
Lemons	1
Chinese eggplant	8 or 9
Plain yogurt	1 cup
Whipping cream	1/2 cup
Chicken	7 whole legs (about 3 1/2 pounds)

SPECIALTY SHOPPING

Basmati rice	2 cups
Chapati flour (Can substitute low-gluten, whole-wheat, pastry-grind flour)	2 cups
Toor daal	1/2 cup
Urid daal	3/4 cup
Chana daal	1/2 cup
Coconut, shredded, unsweetened	3/4 cup
Tamarind Concentrate	6 x 4-inch piece
Curry leaves	4 sprigs
Coconut milk	2 cups

Alu Bonda (Deep-Fried Spicy Potato Balls with Peanut Mint Cilantro Chutney)

Feast from
South India

APPETIZER
Alu Bonda (Deep-Fried Spicy Potato Balls with Peanut Mint Cilantro Chutney)

MAIN DISH
Chicken Mulligatawney (A Chicken Curry from Tamilnadu)

SIDE DISH
Vendaka Masala Pachdi (Okra with Tomatoes, Onions, Coconut Milk and Spices)

RICE DISH
Kadugu Sadam (Mustard Seed Rice)

BREAD
Poori (Deep-Fried Puffy Bread)

DESSERT
Semiya Payasam (Vermicelli Pudding)

SOUTH INDIA INCLUDES FOUR STATES: Karnataka and Kerala on the west coast and Tamilnadu and Andhra Pradesh on the east coast. While each of these states has its own cuisine, they share many common characteristics. Coconut grows abundantly in all of South India and is used liberally in cooking. Rice also grows abundantly and is eaten as a staple.

South Indian cuisine gets its distinguishing flavors from the use of curry leaves, fenugreek seeds, fennel, tamarind and asafetida. South Indian dishes are generally spiced more robustly and are hotter than food from North India. The state of Andhra Pradesh boasts the hottest food, and the state of Kerala is a close second. The south remained largely untouched by Muslim invaders and this is also reflected in the cuisine, which tends to be mostly vegetarian. In southern coastal areas, seafood, especially shellfish, features prominently.

Alu Bonda (Deep-Fried Spicy Potato Balls with Peanut Mint Cilantro Chutney)

INGREDIENTS (Serves 6)

2 tablespoons oil

2 teaspoons black mustard seeds

2 tablespoons finely chopped ginger

1 dry red chile pepper, broken into 4 to 5 pieces (optional)

1 tablespoon urid *daal

7 to 8 fresh curry leaves (optional)

1/2 medium onion, finely chopped

1/2 teaspoon turmeric

1 teaspoon salt

1/2 cup frozen peas (thawed) or fresh peas (boiled)

3 medium potatoes, boiled, peeled and cut into 1/4-inch dice

1/4 cup cashew pieces

2 tablespoons lemon juice

1 cup loosely packed chickpea flour

1/2 cup plus 2 tablespoons water

1/2 teaspoon salt

3/4 teaspoon baking powder

Oil for deep-frying

*see "daal" in chapter 2, "Indian Ingredients and Spices"

1. Heat 2 tablespoons oil in a 6-quart saucepot. When hot, add mustard seeds, ginger, chile pepper, urid daal and curry leaves. Sauté for about 30 seconds and then add chopped onion. Sauté onion over medium-high heat for about 4 to 5 minutes. Add turmeric, salt and peas, and cook for another 2 minutes. Add potatoes, cashew pieces, and lemon juice; mix thoroughly, remove from heat and let cool. Divide into twelve portions. Form each portion into a small ball by rolling between your hands. Set aside.

2. In a 3- to 4-quart bowl, mix together chickpea flour, water, salt and baking powder to form a batter the consistency of thick buttermilk. Set aside.

3. In a frying pan, heat oil to 325 degrees. When oil is hot, dip potato balls in batter and then deep-fry about six at a time over medium to medium-high heat until the balls are crispy and golden brown. Balls may need to be turned for even frying. Drain on paper towels and serve with Peanut Mint Cilantro Chutney.

Making Alu Bonda (Deep-Fried Spicy Potato Balls)

Peanut Mint Cilantro Chutney

1 large tomato, coarsely chopped

1/2 medium onion, coarsely chopped

1 1/2 cups loosely packed cilantro leaves

1/2 cup mint leaves (about 1/2 bunch)

1/2 teaspoon salt

1/4 cup roasted peanuts

3 to 4 teaspoons Tamarind Concentrate (see page 26)

1 serrano chile pepper, about 3 inches long, chopped (optional)

Hot chile pepper powder, to taste (optional)

Puree tomato and onion in a blender until liquid. Add and puree the remaining ingredients gradually with the blender running. Taste and adjust for salt and tamarind. If a hotter version is desired, add some hot chile pepper powder. The chutney can be prepared ahead and refrigerated. Leftover chutney can be frozen (for up to a month) and thawed for later use.

Chicken Mulligatawney
(Chicken Curry from Tamilnadu)

The word mulligatawney *is a Tamil word derived from* mulligat, *which means peppercorns. Many Indian restaurants in this country offer mulligatawney soup. In India, we also have mulligatawny curries. Chicken Mulligatawney—curry—is my wife's favorite dish. She insisted that we serve it at our wedding reception.*

INGREDIENTS (Serves 6)

3 tablespoons oil

1-inch piece ginger, chopped

6 to 8 cloves garlic, chopped

3 dried red chile peppers, broken in pieces

3 medium onions, cut in quarters and thinly sliced

2 pounds deboned and skinned chicken dark meat, cut into 1- to 2-inch pieces

2 medium potatoes, peeled and cut into 1-inch cubes

2 teaspoons coriander powder

1 teaspoon turmeric

2 teaspoons white poppy seeds

1 teaspoon paprika

1/2 to 2 teaspoons hot chile pepper powder

1 1/2 teaspoons fennel powder

2 teaspoons black peppercorns

1 1/2 teaspoons cumin powder

1 1/2 teaspoons salt, or to taste

1 cup coconut milk

1/4 cup curry leaves

2 tablespoons lime juice

1 teaspoon Garam Masala (see page 24)

1. Heat the oil in a 6- to 8-quart nonstick saucepan. When hot, add ginger, garlic and chile peppers. Fry for 10 to 15 seconds.

2. Add onions and sauté over medium-high heat, stirring every 2 to 3 minutes, until slightly brown, about 10 minutes.

3. Turn to high heat. When pan is hot, add chicken and stir until all the chicken pieces are nicely browned. Continue browning until most of the moisture has evaporated.

4. Add cubed potatoes and all of the spices and salt; cook for about 3 to 4 minutes. Add coconut milk and bring the mixture to a boil. Reduce heat and add curry leaves, then cover and simmer for 20 minutes, or until the chicken is tender. Mix in lime juice and Garam Masala.

Chicken Mulligatawney (Chicken Curry from Tamilnadu)

Vendaka Masala Pachdi (Okra with Tomatoes, Onions, Coconut Milk and Spices)

At Ajanta a large number of customers anxiously look forward to this dish every summer. We feature it only during July and August, when locally grown fresh okra becomes available.

INGREDIENTS (Serves 6)

5 tablespoons oil, divided

1 1/2 teaspoons mustard seeds

1 teaspoon cumin seeds

2 dry red chiles, broken in pieces

2 tablespoons urid daal*

1 1/2 medium onions, chopped

2 medium tomatoes, chopped

3 teaspoons coriander powder

1 teaspoon turmeric

1 teaspoon paprika

1/2 to 2 teaspoons hot chile pepper powder, to taste

1 1/2 teaspoons salt

3/4 cup coconut milk

3/4 cup yogurt

1/2 cup ground cashews

10 to 12 curry leaves

2 pounds okra

*see "daal" in chapter 2, "Indian Ingredients and Spices"

1. Heat 2 tablespoons oil in a 6- to 8-quart nonstick saucepot. When hot, add mustard seeds, cumin seeds, red chiles and urid daal. Fry for about 30 seconds.

2. Add onions and sauté over medium-high heat until they become soft, about 8 to 10 minutes. Add tomatoes, spices and salt, and cook, stirring occasionally, for about 4 to 5 minutes. Add coconut milk, yogurt, ground cashews and curry leaves. Cook over medium heat for about 20 to 25 minutes, partially covered. The sauce should begin to thicken. If the sauce is not thick, remove the cover and cook over high heat a few minutes. The finished sauce should be the consistency of porridge.

3. Cut off and discard the inedible top of each okra; also cut off 1/4 inch from the bottom. Slice the okra in 1/2- to 3/4-inch slices. In a large skillet, heat the remaining three tablespoons of oil. Sauté the sliced okra over high heat for about 12 to 15 minutes, stirring once every two to three minutes. Add the sauce and cook another 5 minutes, or until okra is cooked.

Vendaka Masala Pachdi (Okra with Tomatoes, Onions, Coconut Milk and Spices)

Kadugu Sadam (Mustard Seed Rice)

INGREDIENTS (Serves 6)

2 cups basmati rice

3 cups water

1/2 cup shredded unsweetened coconut

1 teaspoon turmeric

2 teaspoons salt

For tempering:
3 tablespoons oil

3 tablespoons urid *daal

1 1/2 tablespoons mustard seeds

15 to 20 curry leaves

3 dry red chiles, broken in pieces

*see "daal" in chapter 2, "Indian Ingredients and Spices"

1. Rinse rice in water two or three times. Drain all the excess water.

2. Bring 3 cups of water to a boil. Add rice, coconut, turmeric and salt. Bring to a boil again. Turn heat to low and simmer until all the moisture is absorbed and the rice is cooked, about 20 minutes. Fluff the rice with a fork.

3. Heat oil for tempering in a small, 1-quart saucepan. When hot, add urid daal and stir-fry until golden brown. Add remaining ingredients and stir for 15 to 30 seconds. When mustard seeds pop, turn off the heat. Add all contents of the saucepan to the rice and mix.

Poori (Deep-Fried Puffy Bread)

This bread puffs up like a balloon when fried and makes an attractive table presentation.

INGREDIENTS (Serves 6)

2 cups chapati or other low-gluten, whole-wheat, pastry-grind flour

1/2 teaspoon salt

1 1/2 tablespoons oil

3/4 to 1 cup water, as needed

Oil for deep-frying

1. Mix all the ingredients except water. Add water gradually, working it into the flour, mixing and kneading. Do not use all the water at once; add it gradually and use only what is necessary. Knead the dough well until it is supple and elastic. The exact quantity of water will vary depending on the type of flour used. Let the dough rest, covered with a damp cloth, for about 30 minutes to 1 hour.

2. In a wok, heat oil for deep-frying. Lower to medium heat once the oil is hot.

3. Divide the dough into sixteen portions and roll each into a small ball. Flatten balls, dust with a little flour and, with a rolling pin, roll them out into circles about 4 to 5 inches in diameter and 1/16 inch thick.

4. Deep-fry the poories until golden brown, turning once to fry on both sides. (See process photos on page 174.) Poori should puff up like a balloon. If this does not happen, the oil is not hot enough. Stop frying and turn up the heat to increase oil temperature before frying more. Place fried poori on a platter lined with paper towels. Serve warm.

Semiya Payasam (Vermicelli Pudding)

Semiya Payasam (Vermicelli Pudding)

INGREDIENTS (Serves 6)

4 cups milk

Seeds from 8 to 10 cardamom pods

1/4 cup butter

3 tablespoons cashew pieces

3 tablespoons raisins

1 cup vermicelli, broken in 1 1/2-inch pieces

1/2 cup sugar

1/2 teaspoon saffron steeped in 3 tablespoons warm milk

1. In a 4- to 6-quart saucepan, bring milk to a boil. Stir frequently with a wire whisk to dislodge milk solids that might stick to the bottom. When milk starts to boil, reduce to medium heat. Simmer over medium heat, stirring until the milk is reduced to three-fourths its original volume, about 20 minutes. Add cardamom seeds and continue simmering gently over low heat.

2. On another burner, melt the butter in a skillet on medium heat. Sauté cashews and raisins for 2 to 3 minutes, or until cashews become golden brown and the raisins puff up. Remove with a slotted spoon and set aside on a plate lined with a paper towel.

3. In the same butter, sauté vermicelli and stir until it is golden brown, about 4 to 5 minutes. Add to the simmering milk, and cook until done, about 10 minutes. Add cashews and raisins. Serve warm.

Making Poori (Deep-Fried Puffy Bread)

South Indian Feast Shopping List

FROM YOUR REFRIGERATOR AND PANTRY

Ginger	3 inch piece
Garlic	8 cloves
Oil	
Sugar	1/2 cup
Whole milk	4 cups
Raisins	3 tablespoons
Cashew pieces	1 1/2 cups
Peanuts, roasted	1/4 cup
Salt	
Frozen peas	1/2 cup
Butter	1/4 cup

SUPERMARKET SHOPPING LIST

Red potatoes	5 medium
Onions	6 medium
Tomatoes	4 medium
Cilantro	1 bunch
Mint	1/2 bunch
Green chile peppers	1
Lemons	1
Lime	1
Okra	2 pounds
Plain yogurt	3/4 cup
Chicken	7 whole legs (About 3 1/2 pounds)

FROM YOUR INDIAN SPICE RACK

Turmeric	3 1/2 teaspoons
Paprika	2 teaspoons
Coriander powder	5 teaspoons
Cumin powder	1 1/2 teaspoons
Hot chile pepper powder	5 teaspoons
Fennel powder	1 1/2 teaspoons
Dry red chile pepper	9
Peppercorns	2 teaspoons
Cumin seeds	1 teaspoon
Black cumin seeds	2 teaspoons
Black mustard seeds	5 teaspoons
Cardamoms	10 pods
Saffron	1/2 teaspoon
White poppy seeds	2 teaspoons
Garam Masala	1 teaspoon

SPECIALTY SHOPPING

Basmati rice	2 cups
Chapati flour (Can substitute low-gluten whole-wheat, pastry-grind flour)	2 cups
Urid daal	6 tablespoons
Curry leaves	10 to 12 sprigs
Chickpea flour	1 cup
Tamarind Concentrate	2 x 2-inch piece
Coconut milk	1 cup + 3/4 cup
Shredded coconut, unsweetened	1/2 cup
Vermicelli	1 cup

Tandoori Asparagus (Spicy Grilled Asparagus)

Additional Appetizer Recipes

Growing up in India, we did not eat appetizers just before dinner or with drinks. We ate them as snacks, usually in the evening, to hold us off until about 9:00 p.m., which was when we usually ate dinner. Whether eaten as snacks or appetizers, these are spicy and very addictive, just like the rest of Indian food.

Tandoori Asparagus (Spicy Grilled Asparagus)

At Ajanta, this is undeniably the most popular appetizer when featured during the spring season. Try it one time, and you will know why. At the restaurant, we cook it in a tandoor oven—a charcoal-fired oven that runs at 1,000 degrees F! At home you can cook it on a grill; it is almost as good.

INGREDIENTS (Serves 4-6)

1 pound asparagus

Marinade:

1/4 cup oil

2 tablespoons lemon juice

1 tablespoon finely minced garlic

1 teaspoon paprika

1 teaspoon salt

1/2 teaspoon clove powder

1 teaspoon toasted ground cumin powder

1. Wash asparagus and let dry. Remove the fibrous, inedible part from the bottom of the asparagus by breaking it off.

2. Mix all the marinade ingredients in a large 6- to 8-quart bowl. Add asparagus and toss gently by hand to coat. Marinate for about 2 hours.

3. Grill the asparagus in a grilling basket on a very hot barbecue about 2 minutes on each side. Serve with Yogurt-Cashew-Sour Cream Sauce (see page 217).

Tandoori Portobello Mushrooms (Spicy Grilled Portobello Mushrooms)

The meaty flavor and the soft texture of this appetizer reminds my wife of foie gras. At the restaurant, we cook it in the extremely hot tandoor oven; at home, I cook it on a hot grill.

INGREDIENTS (Serves 4-6)

4 Portobello mushrooms

Marinade:

1/4 cup oil

2 tablespoons lemon juice

1 tablespoon finely minced ginger

1 teaspoon paprika

1 teaspoon salt

1/2 teaspoon toasted ground clove powder

1/2 teaspoon toasted ground cinnamon powder

1/2 teaspoon toasted ground cardamom powder

1. Remove stems from mushrooms and slice the caps in 1/2-inch-thick strips, about 4 to 5 strips per mushroom.

2. Mix all the marinade ingredients in a large 4- to 6-quart bowl. Add mushroom strips and gently toss to coat, making sure they do not break. Marinate for 1 to 2 hours.

3. Grill the mushrooms in a grilling basket on a very hot barbecue about 2 to 3 minutes on each side. Serve with Yogurt-Cashew-Tamarind Sauce (see page 217).

Tandoori Portobello Mushrooms (Spicy Grilled Portobello Mushrooms)

Sabzi Tikki (Mixed Vegetable Cakes)

INGREDIENTS (Serves 6)

2 to 3 medium-size red potatoes, boiled, peeled and mashed (about 1 1/2 cups mashed)

2 slices white bread, crust removed, processed into bread crumbs

1-inch piece ginger, peeled and finely diced

2 teaspoons ajwain seeds

1/4 cup loosely packed chopped cilantro or dill

1 teaspoon salt

1 teaspoon chile flakes

1 green chile pepper, finely chopped

1/2 cup each: grated cauliflower, grated carrots and cooked peas

Oil for shallow frying

1. Thoroughly mix all the ingredients in a bowl. Divide into twelve equal parts. Form each part in to a cake about 2 to 3 inches in diameter and 1/2 inch thick.

2. Heat the oil about 1/4 inch deep in a skillet. When very hot, pan-fry 3 to 4 cakes at a time about 2 minutes on each side, or until golden brown. Do not fry too many cakes at one time. The oil temperature will drop and the cakes will fall apart or soak up too much oil. Serve with Mint Cilantro Chutney (see recipe on page 47).

Khumbi Pakora (Portobello Mushroom Fritters)

These fritters made with Portobello are not very Indian, but truly delicious.

INGREDIENTS (Serves 4-6)

1/2 cup loosely packed besan (chickpea flour)

1/2 cup loosely packed rice flour

1/2 teaspoon salt

1 teaspoon ajwain seeds

1/2 teaspoon crushed chile peppers

1/2 cup water

1 teaspoon baking powder

2 Portobello mushrooms (about 1/2 pound), cut in 1/2-inch-thick strips and then cut in 1- to 11/2-inch-long pieces

Oil for deep-frying

1. Mix the first seven ingredients in a 4-quart bowl, using a whisk to make a smooth batter.

2. Heat the oil in a frying pan to a temperature of about 325 degrees. Dip strips of mushrooms in the batter and deep-fry until golden brown. Remove and place on a plate lined with paper towels. Fry about 6 to 8 strips at a time, making sure the oil remains very hot, otherwise, the Pakora will absorb too much oil. Continue frying in batches until all the strips are done. Serve with Yogurt-Cashew-Tamarind Sauce (see page 217).

Khumbi Pakora (Portobello Mushroom Fritters)

Malabar Chicken Curry

Additional Chicken Recipes

These chicken recipes can be substituted for the main course in any of the feast menus, or you may design a menu of your own with a chicken dish as the main entree.

Malabar Chicken Curry

This dish originates from the Malabar Coast, which spans the west coast states of Karnataka and Kerala in South India. This is a light curry with robust flavors. It is eaten hot in South India.

INGREDIENTS (Serves 4-6)

3 tablespoons oil

2 teaspoons mustard seeds

1-inch piece ginger, chopped

3 to 4 dried red chiles, broken in pieces

3 medium onions, quartered and thinly sliced

2 pounds boneless, skinless chicken dark meat, cut in 1- to 2-inch pieces

2 teaspoons coriander powder

1 teaspoon turmeric powder

2 teaspoons paprika

1/2 to 2 teaspoons hot chile pepper powder, to taste

2 teaspoons fennel powder

1 1/2 teaspoons black peppercorns

1 1/2 teaspoons salt

1 cup coconut milk

2 medium potatoes, peeled and cut into 3/4-inch cubes

8 to 10 curry leaves

1. In a 6- to 8-quart saucepot, heat the oil. When hot, add mustard seeds. Fry for about 10 to 15 seconds. When mustard seeds pop, add ginger and broken red chiles and fry for another 15 seconds.

2. Add onions and sauté over medium to high heat until slightly brown, about 10 to 12 minutes. Raise the heat to high and wait 1 to 2 minutes, or until the pan gets very hot. Add chicken and stir-fry until almost all the moisture has dried up and the chicken is nicely browned.

3. Reduce heat to medium; add all the spices and salt. Stir for 3 to 4 minutes and then add coconut milk (shake can before opening). Bring the mixture to a boil; add 1/4 cup water if there is not enough liquid. Reduce heat, add potatoes, cover and simmer slowly for about 20 to 25 minutes, or until chicken and potatoes are tender. Add curry leaves during the last 5 minutes of cooking.

Kozi Milagu Chettinad (Chicken in Black Pepper Sauce)

This dish comes from the deep southern region of Tamilnadu and showcases peppercorns, which grow abundantly in this area. Chefs from the Chettinad community are well known all over India, and food from this area is highly seasoned, very aromatic and rich.

INGREDIENTS (Serves 4-6)

3 tablespoons oil

1 1/2-inch piece ginger, peeled and chopped

8 to 10 cloves garlic, chopped

3 medium onions, quartered and sliced less than 1/16 inch thick

2 pounds deboned and skinned chicken dark meat, cut in 1- to 2- inch pieces

1 1/2 teaspoons turmeric powder

3 teaspoons coriander powder

2 1/2 tablespoons freshly ground black pepper powder

1 1/2 teaspoons salt, or to taste

3 medium tomatoes, chopped

1 1/2 cups plain yogurt

8 to 10 curry leaves

2 teaspoon Garam Masala (see page 24)

3 tablespoons lemon juice

1. Heat the oil in a thick 6- to 8-quart saucepot. When hot, add ginger and garlic. Fry for about 10 to 15 seconds. Add onions and sauté over medium to high heat until slightly browned, about 10 to 12 minutes. Raise heat to high. When the pot gets very hot, add chicken and stir-fry until the chicken pieces are browned and excess moisture has evaporated.

2. Reduce heat to medium, add all the spices (except Garam Masala) and salt. Stir for about 3 to 4 minutes and then add tomatoes and yogurt. Bring the mixture to a boil. Reduce heat, cover and simmer slowly for about 15 to 20 minutes, or until chicken is tender. Add curry leaves, Garam Masala and lemon juice during the last 5 minutes of cooking.

Kozi Milagu Chettinad (Chicken in Black Pepper Sauce)

Kandahari Chicken

This is a Moghlai chicken curry named after Kandahar, a major city in Afghanistan. The distinctive feature of this dish is its use of pomegranate juice, an Afghan influence on Indian cooking. The pomegranate juice gives the sauce a pleasant sweet-and-sour taste.

INGREDIENTS (Serves 4-6)

3 tablespoons oil

8 medium cloves garlic, chopped

3 medium onions, quartered and thinly sliced

2 pounds skinned and deboned chicken dark meat, cut in 1- to 2-inch pieces

3 medium tomatoes, pureed

1 teaspoon paprika

1/2 to 2 teaspoons chile peppers, to taste

4 teaspoons cumin powder

1 1/2 teaspoons salt

3/4 cup ground cashews

1 cup pomegranate juice

3/4 cup cream

2 teaspoons Garam Masala (see page 24)

1. Heat the oil in a 6- to 8-quart saucepot. When hot, add garlic and sauté for about 15 seconds. Add onions and sauté over high heat for about 10 to 12 minutes, or until the onions become light golden brown.

2. Raise heat to high and wait for 1 to 2 minutes, or until the pan gets hot. Add chicken and quickly stir-fry until it is browned and most of the moisture has evaporated. Add pureed tomatoes and all the spices (except Garam Masala), salt, cashews and pomegranate juice. Bring the mixture to a boil and then reduce to a simmer. Simmer over low heat, uncovered, about 20 minutes, or until the chicken is tender. Stir in the cream and sprinkle Garam Masala on top.

Chicken Pistachio Korma

Undoubtedly a rich sauce is what makes this Moghlai dish so popular whenever it is featured on the menu at Ajanta. We get many requests to make it a permanent menu item.

INGREDIENTS (Serves 4-6)

3 tablespoons oil

6 to 8 cloves of garlic, finely chopped

4 medium onions, cut in 6 pieces vertically and then sliced 1/16 inch thick

2 pounds deboned and skinned chicken dark meat, cut into 1- to 2-inch pieces

2 teaspoons ground cumin

2 teaspoons turmeric

2 teaspoons white pepper powder

1 1/2 teaspoons salt, or to taste

1 cup plain yogurt

1/2 cup ground pistachios

1/2 cup ground cashews

1 cup cilantro, ground in food processor

1/2 cup heavy cream

2 teaspoons Garam Masala (see page 24)

1. Heat the oil in a 6- to 8-quart saucepot. When hot, add garlic and sauté for about 10 to 15 seconds. Add onions and sauté, stirring every 1 to 2 minutes, over medium-high heat for about 10 to 12 minutes, or until onions become translucent and slightly brown.

2. Raise heat to high. Add chicken pieces and stir-fry until they are browned and most the moisture has evaporated. Reduce heat to medium, add spices (except Garam Masala) and salt and continue sautéing for about 3 minutes.

3. Add yogurt, pistachios, cashews and cilantro. Raise heat and bring the mixture to a boil. Reduce heat, cover and simmer for about 20 minutes, or until chicken is cooked through and becomes tender.

Marzwangan Korma (Lamb Cooked in Red Pepper and Tamarind Sauce)

Additional Lamb Recipes

These lamb recipes can be substituted for the main course in any of the feast menus, or you may design a menu of your own with a lamb dish as the main entrée.

Tamil Lamb Curry

A lamb curry from Tamilnadu, in South India.

INGREDIENTS (Serves 4-6)

3 teaspoons cumin seeds

2 teaspoons black peppercorns

3 teaspoons whole coriander seeds

1 1/2 teaspoons fennel seeds

3 teaspoons white poppy seeds

2 tablespoons water

1/4 cup oil

1-inch piece ginger, scraped and chopped

6 to 8 cloves garlic, peeled and chopped

3 medium onions, quartered and thinly sliced

2 pounds boneless lamb, defatted and cubed (weigh after defatting)

1 teaspoon turmeric

2 teaspoons paprika

1/2 to 2 teaspoons hot chile pepper powder, to taste

2 teaspoons salt, or to taste

3 medium tomatoes, chopped coarsely and pureed

1 cup coconut milk

3 tablespoons Tamarind Concentrate (see page 26)

2 to 3 sprigs curry leaves (optional)

1. In a dry skillet, toast together cumin, peppercorns, coriander, fennel and poppy seeds, stirring frequently for 3 to 4 minutes or until the spices seem to be toasted and dehydrated. Transfer to a blender, add water gradually and grind together into a paste. Add just enough water to make a thick paste. Set aside.

2. In a 6- to 8-quart saucepot, heat oil. When hot, add ginger and garlic, and sauté for about 20 seconds. Add onions and sauté over medium to high heat, stirring occasionally, for 10 to 12 minutes or until the onions are soft and slightly brown.

3. Turn the heat to high, and add the cubed lamb and sauté, stirring frequently, until the lamb is nicely browned. Continue sautéing until most of the moisture is evaporated. Reduce heat to medium, add all the spices (including the spice paste) and salt. Sauté for 3 to 4 minutes, and then add pureed tomatoes and coconut milk. Bring to a boil, reduce heat, cover and simmer over low heat for 30 to 40 minutes, or until the lamb becomes tender. Add and mix in tamarind concentrate and curry leaves during the last 5 minutes.

Marzwangan Korma (Lamb Cooked in Red Pepper and Tamarind Sauce)

A lamb dish from the state of Kashmir.

INGREDIENTS (Serves 4-6)

3 tablespoons oil

2 pounds boneless lamb, defatted and cut in 1- to 2-inch cubes

5 large red bell peppers, stems and seeds removed, coarsely chopped and pureed

1 1/2 teaspoons salt

3 teaspoons paprika powder

1 to 2 teaspoons hot chile pepper powder

3 teaspoons fennel powder

1 1/2 teaspoons turmeric

1 1/2 teaspoons dry ginger powder

4 tablespoons Tamarind Concentrate (see page 26)

2 teaspoon Garam Masala (see page 24)

1/2 cup whipping cream

1. Heat the oil in a 6- to 8-quart saucepot. When hot, add cubed lamb and stir until the lamb is nicely browned and all the excess moisture is evaporated.

2. Add pureed bell pepper, salt and all the spices except Garam Masala. Bring to a boil, reduce heat, cover and simmer until the lamb becomes tender, about 30 to 40 minutes.

Gradually add tamarind concentrate, taste and stop adding tamarind when the sauce tastes pleasantly sour. Stir in the Garam Masala and turn off the heat. Add and mix whipping cream.

Achari Gosht (Lamb Curry with Indian Pickling Spices)

A lamb dish from North India, known for its tart, spicy sauce.

INGREDIENTS (Serves 4-6)

3 tablespoons mustard oil (or vegetable oil)

2 teaspoons cumin seeds

2 teaspoons mustard seeds

2 teaspoons nigella seeds

2 teaspoons fenugreek seeds

2 teaspoons fennel seeds

1-inch piece ginger, peeled and finely chopped

6 to 8 cloves garlic, peeled and chopped

3 medium onions, quartered and thinly sliced

2 pounds boneless cubed lamb, defatted (weigh after deboning and defatting)

1 1/2 teaspoons turmeric powder

1 1/2 teaspoons salt

2 teaspoons paprika

1 to 2 teaspoons hot chile pepper powder, to taste

3 teaspoons coriander powder

1 cup plain yogurt

3 tablespoons lemon juice

1. Heat the oil in a 6- to 8-quart saucepot. When hot, add cumin seeds, mustard seeds, nigella seeds, fenugreek seeds and fennel seeds. When the seeds pop, add ginger and garlic. Fry for about 15 seconds.

2. Add onions and sauté over medium-high heat, stirring frequently, until the onions become slightly brown.

3. Raise to high heat. When the pot becomes very hot, add lamb and

sauté until the lamb is nicely browned and most of the moisture is evaporated. Add turmeric, salt, paprika, chile powder and coriander powder. Stir-fry for 2 to 3 minutes. Turn the heat off, mix in yogurt, and turn the heat back. This is done to prevent the yogurt from curdling.

4. Bring the mixture to a boil (add some water, 1/4 to 1/2 cup, if there is not enough liquid), reduce heat and simmer over low heat, without covering the pan, for 30 to 40 minutes, or until lamb becomes tender. At this time, you will notice a thin film of oil on the top surface. Add lemon juice.

Ilaichi Gosht (Lamb in Cardamom Sauce)

A lamb dish from state of Sindh.

INGREDIENTS (Serves 4-6)

3 tablespoons oil

3 medium onions, quartered and thinly sliced

1 green chile pepper, chopped

2 pounds boneless cubed lamb, defatted (weigh after defatting)

3 teaspoons coriander powder

2 to 3 teaspoons freshly ground black peppercorns, to taste

3 teaspoons freshly ground toasted cardamoms

2 teaspoons ginger powder

1 1/2 teaspoons salt

1 cup plain yogurt

1/2 cup cashews, ground

1. Heat the oil in a 6- to 8-quart saucepot. When hot, add onions and green chile pepper, and sauté over medium-high heat, stirring frequently, until the onions become golden brown.

2. Raise to high heat. When the pan becomes hot, add cubed lamb and sauté until the lamb is nicely browned and most of the moisture is evaporated. Add all the spices and salt. Stir-fry for 2 to 3 minutes, then add yogurt and ground cashews.

3. Bring the mixture to a boil (add about 1/4 cup water if there is not enough liquid), reduce heat, cover and simmer over low heat for about 45 minutes, or until lamb becomes tender.

Jhinga Bhuna Masala (Prawns in a Thick, Spicy Sauce)

Additional Seafood Recipes

These seafood recipes can be substituted for the main dish in any of the feast menus, or you may design a menu of your own with a seafood dish as the main entrée.

Jhinga Bhuna Masala (Prawns in a Thick, Spicy Sauce)

This is my favorite prawn recipe. I like the layers and layers of flavors due to a multitude of ingredients. The flavors become concentrated because of the sauce reduction.

INGREDIENTS (Serves 4-6)

1/4 cup oil

2 teaspoons mustard seeds

3 to 4 dried red chiles, broken into 1/4-inch pieces

2-inch piece ginger, scraped and chopped

8 to 10 medium cloves garlic, finely chopped

2 medium onions chopped

4 medium tomatoes, cut in 1/4-inch dice

1 to 2 green chiles, seeded and chopped

3 teaspoons coriander seeds, pounded with a pestle or coarsely ground

1 1/2 teaspoons salt, or to taste

1 teaspoon turmeric

2 teaspoons paprika

1/2 to 2 teaspoons hot chile pepper powder, to taste

2 teaspoons ajwain

1 1/2 tablespoons dried fenugreek herb

2 pounds jumbo shrimp, peeled and deveined

3 tablespoons lemon juice

1/2 cup loosely packed chopped cilantro

1. Heat the oil in a large skillet. When hot, add mustard seeds, red chiles, ginger and garlic. Stir and sauté for about 30 seconds.

2. Add onions. Sauté over high heat for 10 minutes, stirring frequently, until the onions become soft and translucent. Add tomatoes and stir-fry 4 to 5 minutes. Reduce to medium heat, add green chiles, coriander seeds, salt, turmeric, paprika, chile pepper powder, and sauté over medium heat for 2 to 3 minutes, or until the oil seems to separate from the mixture. Add ajwain and fenugreek. Mix and cook until the mixture is thick and has very little moisture left.

3. Raise to high heat and add shrimp. Stir and cook for 2 to 3 minutes, or until the shrimp is cooked. Do not overcook the shrimp. The shrimp should become opaque but still look plump. Add lemon juice and cilantro. Mix and remove from heat.

Prawn Curry Bengal

An easy-to-prepare prawn curry from Bengal.

INGREDIENTS (Serves 4-6)

1/4 cup oil, divided	2 teaspoons turmeric
1 teaspoon fenugreek seeds	1/2 to 2 teaspoons chile pepper powder, to taste
1 teaspoon ajwain seeds	
1 teaspoon black or yellow mustard seeds	1 teaspoon paprika
	3 teaspoons cumin powder
1 teaspoon nigella seeds	3 medium tomatoes, pureed
6 to 8 medium cloves garlic, chopped	1 3/4 cups coconut milk
1/2 pound shallots, chopped	1 1/2 teaspoons salt, or to taste
1 chopped green chile pepper (optional)	2 pounds large prawns, peeled and deveined

1. In a 6- to 8-quart saucepot, heat 2 tablespoons oil. When very hot, add fenugreek seeds, ajwain seeds, mustard seeds and nigella seeds (oil should be hot enough to it sizzle when seeds are added; test by dropping a couple of seeds in first). Sauté seeds for about 10 seconds and then add garlic. Stir and sauté garlic for about 15 seconds.

2. Add chopped shallots and sauté for 6 to 8 minutes over medium to high heat. Add green chile pepper, and all the spices, and sauté for another 2 to 3 minutes. Add tomatoes, coconut milk and salt, and cook over medium heat, partially covered, for about 20 minutes. Adjust heat level and leave the sauce simmering over low heat. The sauce should be the consistency of buttermilk. If it is too thick, add some water. If it is too watery, remove the lid and boil off some of the moisture.

3. In an 8- to 10-inch skillet, heat the remaining 2 tablespoons oil. When very hot, almost to the smoking point, add prawns and stir-fry for about 2 minutes, or until the prawns change color. Add the sauce, and mix and cook another 1 to 2 minutes, or until the prawns are cooked through.

Note: Step number 3 can be done just before you are ready to sit down and eat. In this case, be sure to turn off the heat under the sauce. Reheat the sauce before adding to the sautéed prawns.

Machi Malai Masala
(Fish in Creamy Curry Sauce)

The sauce gets its creamy quality from the yogurt and coconut milk used in the sauce.

INGREDIENTS (Serves 4-6)

6 tablespoons oil, divided

8 to 10 cloves garlic, chopped

1-inch piece ginger, peeled and chopped

3 medium onions, cut in quarters and thinly sliced

2 teaspoons mustard seeds

2 teaspoons turmeric

2 teaspoons paprika

1/2 to 2 teaspoons hot chile pepper powder, to taste

2 teaspoons salt

1 cup plain yogurt

1 cup coconut milk

1 1/2 teaspoons Garam Masala (see page 24)

2 pounds fish fillet (halibut or catfish), cut into 2 x 2-inch pieces

1. Heat 3 tablespoons oil in a large skillet. When hot, add garlic and

ginger. Sauté for about 30 seconds and then add the onions. Sauté over high heat until soft, about 12 to 15 minutes. Transfer to a food processor and coarsely grind the onions.

2. Heat 1 tablespoon oil in a 6- to 8-quart saucepot. When very hot, add mustard seeds. When seeds pop, add the ground onions. Add all the spices (except Garam Masala) and salt. Sauté over high heat for 3 to 4 minutes. Add yogurt and coconut milk, reduce heat and simmer for

about 20 to 25 minutes, until the oil separates from the mixture and forms a thin layer on top of the sauce. Add Garam Masala.

3. In a separate skillet, heat remaining oil. When hot to the point of smoking, add fish and sauté for about 1 minute on each side. Transfer fish to the curry sauce in the saucepan and simmer for 1 to 2 minutes, or until the fish is cooked and flakes off easily.

Methi Machi (Fish Cooked in Fenugreek Herb Sauce)

I developed this recipe based on my memory of how my mom cooked this dish. When I was growing up, this was one of my favorite dishes. It is also very popular at Ajanta whenever it is featured.

INGREDIENTS (Serves 4-6)

6 tablespoons oil, divided

6 to 8 cloves garlic, chopped

1-inch piece ginger, peeled and chopped

2 medium onions, finely chopped

5 medium tomatoes, pureed

1 green chile pepper, chopped

2 teaspoons coriander powder

1 teaspoon paprika

1/2 to 1 teaspoon hot chile pepper powder, to taste

1 teaspoon cumin powder

1 teaspoon turmeric

4 tablespoons dried fenugreek herb*

1 cup loosely packed chopped cilantro

1/2 cup loosely packed chopped dill

1 1/2 teaspoons salt, to taste

3 tablespoons lemon juice

2 pounds fresh halibut fillet (or other white fish), cut into 2 x 2-inch pieces

*Crumble store-bought dried fenugreek between your fingers and remove any sticks, etc.

1. In a large skillet, heat 3 tablespoons oil. When hot, add garlic and ginger. The oil should be hot enough so that the garlic and ginger sizzle when dropped in. Sauté for about 10 to 15 seconds. Add onions and sauté for about 10 to 12 minutes over medium to high heat.

2. Add pureed tomatoes. Cook for about 5 minutes. Add green chile pepper, spices, fenugreek, cilantro, dill and salt. Mix and cook over medium heat partially covered for 25 to 30 minutes, or until the sauce becomes the consistency of a thick paste. Stir every 3 to 4 minutes, making sure that the sauce does not stick to the bottom of the pot and burn. If the sauce seems to stick to the bottom of the pan, reduce the heat. If there is too much moisture, remove the lid.

On the other hand, if there is too little moisture, cook with the pot completely covered. Add lemon juice, mix and keep the sauce warm at very low heat.

3. Heat the remaining oil in another skillet. When very hot, almost to the smoking point, add halibut pieces and quickly sauté for about 1 minute on each side, making sure that the fish changes color. Remove the fish with a slotted spoon and add to the sauce in the first skillet. Heat the sauce and cook the fish over medium heat until it is cooked and flakes off easily. The cooking time will depend on the thickness of the fillets.

Methi Machi (Fish Cooked in Fenugreek Herb Sauce)

Bheh, Khumbi Aur Matar (Lotus Root, Mushrooms and Peas in a Caramelized Onion Sauce)

❖ Additional ❖
Vegetarian Recipes

These vegetarian recipes can be substituted in any of the feast menus, or you may design your own feast of vegetarian recipes.

Urid Daal

Daals are dishes made with lentils or legumes. Daals make excellent side dishes and provide protein in a vegetarian meal. Urid daal is known for its creamy quality and is my favorite among all the daals.

INGREDIENTS (Serves 6)

1 cup urid daal	1 large tomato, chopped
5 to 6 cups water	2 to 3 tablespoons Tamarind Concentrate (see page 26)
1 teaspoon salt, or to taste	
1 teaspoon turmeric	1/3 cup loosely packed chopped fresh cilantro
2 tablespoons oil	1 green chile pepper, chopped (optional)
2 teaspoons cumin seeds	

1. Pick over daal and remove pieces of stone or any foreign objects. Wash daal two or three times in water. Heat the water and the daal together in a large 6- to 8-quart saucepot. Bring to a boil, reduce heat and simmer, uncovered; use a sieve to remove any scum or foam that may form on top. Add salt and turmeric after about 30 minutes of boiling. Simmer covered over low heat for another 45 minutes or so, checking to make sure the daal is cooked. Add more water, if necessary. On the other hand, if there seems to be too much moisture, cook uncovered for a while. The final product should be quite thick, almost yogurt-like in consistency.

2. In a 1-quart saucepan, heat the oil. When very hot, add cumin seeds. Fry the seeds until they pop, about 20 seconds, then add to the daal. Add the remaining ingredients. Mix and cook about 5 more minutes.

Lobhia Aur Khumbi (Black-Eyed Peas and Mushrooms)

This dish from Punjab is featured every winter on the menu at Ajanta. We receive more requests to bring back this dish than any other dish.

INGREDIENTS (Serves 4-6)

1/4 cup oil, divided

2 teaspoons cumin seeds

6 cloves garlic, peeled and chopped

2 medium onions, finely chopped

4 medium tomatoes, chopped

3 teaspoons coriander powder

3 teaspoons cumin powder

1 teaspoon paprika

1/2 to 2 teaspoons hot chile pepper powder, to taste

2 teaspoons turmeric

2 teaspoons salt

2-pound packet of frozen black-eyed peas or 4 pounds fresh black-eyed peas, shelled*

3/4 cup water

1 pound shiitake mushrooms, stems removed, sliced into 1/4-inch-thick slices

1 teaspoon Garam Masala (see page 24)

1/4 cup loosely packed chopped cilantro

*Weigh before shelling.

1. In a 6- to 8-quart saucepot, heat 2 tablespoons oil. When hot, add cumin seeds. When seeds pop, add garlic and stir-fry for 10 to 15 seconds. Add onions and sauté for 8 to 10 minutes over high heat, or until onions become soft and translucent. Add tomatoes and cook for about 5 minutes. Add all the spices (except Garam Masala) and salt, stir and cook another 5 minutes.

2. Add black-eyed peas and water, bring the mixture to a boil, reduce heat, cover and simmer over medium heat for about 40 to 50 minutes, or until the peas are tender.

3. In a skillet, heat remaining oil. When hot, add sliced mushrooms and sauté for about 3 to 4 minutes.

4. Add sautéed mushrooms to the black-eyed peas. Add Garam Masala and chopped cilantro, and cook for about 4 to 5 minutes.

Bheh, Khumbi Aur Matar
(Lotus Root, Mushrooms and Peas in a Caramelized Onion Sauce)

This dish offers a wonderful combination of textures and flavors: soft mushrooms, hard and crunchy lotus root, sweet caramelized onions and tart mango powder.

INGREDIENTS (Serves 4-6)

1 1/2 pounds lotus root

3 tablespoons oil

2-inch piece ginger, peeled and chopped

4 medium onions, quartered and thinly sliced

3 teaspoons coriander powder

2 teaspoons cumin powder

2 teaspoons turmeric powder

3 teaspoons mango powder

2 teaspoons paprika powder

1/2 to 2 teaspoons hot chile pepper powder, to taste

2 teaspoons salt

1 cup green peas, frozen

1/2 pound shiitake mushrooms, stems removed, caps cut in half

---

1. Peel lotus root and cut off ends. If necessary, cut into 3- to 4-inch pieces, unless that is the natural size of the root. Boil for about 1 1/2 hours, until the lotus root is tender. Let cool. Cut in half along the length, then cut in 1/8-inch-thick slices. Set aside.

2. Heat the oil in a 6- to 8-quart saucepot. When hot, add ginger. Stir-fry for about 10 to 15 seconds. Add onions and sauté over high heat for about 20 to 25 minutes, stirring frequently, or until the onions are dark golden brown. Add all the spices and salt, reduce heat and stir-fry for about 10 minutes.

3. Add sliced lotus root, peas and mushrooms, and stir-fry another 5 minutes.

Bharwan Bhindi
(Spicy Stuffed Okra)

Stuffed okra is prepared in many ways throughout India. The following recipe from the state of Sindh is a favorite family recipe.

INGREDIENTS (Serves 4-6)

1 1/2 pounds okra

3 teaspoons coriander powder

1 1/2 teaspoons turmeric

1 teaspoon paprika

1/2 to 2 teaspoons hot chile pepper powder, to taste

2 teaspoons mango powder

1 1/2 teaspoons salt

1/4 cup oil

1. Cut, remove and throw away the inedible top portion and about 1/8 inch from the bottom of each okra. Make a slit along the length of each okra, with the knife not slicing deeper than 3/4 inch of the thickness of the okra. In a small bowl, mix all the spices and salt together. Fill or stuff a large pinch of the spice mixture in each okra by opening the slit.

2. Heat the oil. When hot, add the spice-filled okra. Stir and cook over medium-high heat until the okra becomes tender, about 15 to 20 minutes.

Making Bharwan Bhind (Spicy Stuffed Okra)

Chicken Biryani

Additional Bread and Rice Recipes

These bread and rice recipes can be substituted in any of the feast menus or served with other entrees.

Masala Paratha (Griddle-Fried Flat Bread Flavored with Spices)

Paratha breads are prepared in many different versions throughout North India. This version is spiced with chile flakes and ajwain.

INGREDIENTS (Serves 4-6)

2 cups chapati flour or other low-gluten whole-wheat pastry-grind flour

3 tablespoons oil for mixing in the dough

1/2 teaspoon salt

3/4 to 1 cup water

Flour for dusting

Oil for griddle frying

2 teaspoons crushed chile peppers

4 teaspoons ajwain

1. In a large bowl, mix the flour, oil and salt. Add water gradually, working it into the flour, mixing and kneading. Do not use all the water at once; add it gradually and use only what is necessary. Knead the dough well until it is supple and elastic. The exact quantity of water will vary depending on the type of flour used. Store in a bowl covered with a damp cloth for about 30 minutes to 1 hour.

2. Heat a griddle on high. Turn the heat down to medium once the griddle is hot.

3. Divide the dough into eight portions. Form each portion into a small ball. Flatten each ball, dust it with a little flour and roll it out into a circle, less than 1/8 inch thick, using a rolling pin. Smear oil or ghee on the top surface of the rolled-out

dough, sprinkle 1/4 teaspoon of crushed chile peppers and 1/2 teaspoon ajwain, and fold in half. Smear more oil or ghee on the folded dough, and fold into a quarter circle. Dust some flour on folded paratha and re-roll it out to less than 1/8 inch thick. The rolled-out paratha will not be a circle.

4. Bake rolled-out paratha on the griddle for about 30 to 40 seconds on each side. Smear the top side with oil or ghee, flip and griddle fry for 20 to 30 seconds. Repeat on the other side. The finished paratha should have golden brown spots on both sides.

Alu Paratha (Griddle-Fried Flat Bread Stuffed with Potatoes)

Another version of paratha bread, stuffed with spiced potatoes.

INGREDIENTS (Serves 4-6)

2 cups chapati flour or other low-gluten whole-wheat pastry-grind flour

3 tablespoons oil for mixing in the dough

1/2 teaspoon salt

3/4 to 1 cup water

Flour for dusting

Potato Mixture:

4 medium potatoes, peeled, boiled and cut in 1/2 inch dice

1 teaspoon salt, for the potatoes

1 green chile pepper, finely chopped (optional)

1/4 cup chopped cilantro (optional)

1 teaspoon chile flakes

Oil for griddle frying

1. In a large bowl, mix the flour, oil and salt. Add water gradually, working it into the flour, mixing and kneading. Do not use all the water at once; add it gradually and use only what is necessary. Knead the dough well until it is supple and elastic. The exact quantity of water will vary depending on the type of flour used. Store in a bowl covered with a damp cloth for 30 minutes to 1 hour.

2. In another bowl, mix together potatoes, salt, chile pepper, cilantro and chileflakes.

3. Heat a griddle on high. Turn the heat down to medium once the griddle is hot.

4. Divide the dough into eight portions and form into small balls.

Flatten each ball, dust it with a little flour and roll it out into a circle about 6 inches in diameter and about 1/8 inch thick, using a rolling pin. Put 1 heaping tablespoon full of potato mixture in the middle of the circle, close the dough around the potatoes, seal it tight and re-roll the dough containing potatoes into a circle, about 7 to 8 inches in diameter.

5. Bake rolled-out paratha on the griddle for about 30 to 40 seconds on each side. Smear the top side with oil or ghee, flip, and griddle fry for 20 to 30 seconds. Repeat on the other side. The finished paratha should have golden brown spots on both sides.

Gajar Aur Matar Ka Pulav (Vegetable Pilaf Made with Carrots and Peas)

Rice pilafs (called "pulav" in India) are prepared in many varieties all over India. This recipe for Vegetable Pilaf, eaten with a raita (see pages 214–15), will make a simple, balanced meal.

INGREDIENTS (Serves 6-8)

2 tablespoons oil	2 teaspoons salt, or to taste
2 teaspoons black cumin seeds	5 to 6 bay leaves
2 cups basmati rice	1 cup peas, fresh or frozen
4 cups water	1 cup grated carrots

1. In a heavy 6- to 8-quart saucepot, heat the oil. When hot, add black cumin seeds. Fry the seeds for about 10 seconds and then add the rice. Sauté the rice for 4 to 5 minutes.

2. Add water, salt and bay leaves. (If using fresh-shelled peas, add these at this time.) Bring to a boil, reduce heat, cover and cook for about 10 minutes. Add peas and grated carrots. Mix, cover and cook another 10 minutes, or until all the liquid is absorbed. Fluff the rice with a fork.

Chicken Biriyani

Biriyanis are very elaborate and very popular Moghlai dishes from India, usually served on special occasions like weddings and graduations. Preparing biriyani involves cooking rice and meats or vegetables together in a steam-tight container by baking. The steam generated by heat cannot escape the container and does the actual cooking. This technique of cooking by steam infuses the flavors deeply and gives a texture to the ingredients that is unique and very appealing. In India, biriyanis are traditionally served with raita (see pages 214–15).

INGREDIENTS (Serves 4-6)

Curry Sauce for Biriyani:

2 tablespoons oil

6 cloves garlic, finely chopped

2 medium onions, chopped

2 teaspoons paprika

1/2 to 2 teaspoons hot chile pepper powder, to taste

1 teaspoon coriander powder

1 teaspoon turmeric powder

2 teaspoons Garam Masala (see page 24)

2 teaspoons salt

3 medium tomatoes, chopped

Chicken for Biriyani:

3 tablespoons oil

1 1/2 pounds boneless and skinless chicken dark meat, cut in 1 1/2- to 2-inch pieces

Toppings for Biriyani:

5 tablespoons oil for caramelizing onions

1/2 cup cashew pieces

1/4 cup raisins

2 medium onions, quartered and thinly sliced

Rice for Biriyani:

1 tablespoon oil

2 teaspoons black cumin seeds

2 cups basmati rice

2 cups water

2 teaspoons salt

2 to 3 cinnamon sticks

5 bay leaves

Dough for sealing Biriyani casserole:

Make Dough by mixing 1/2 cup flour and 3 to 4 tablespoons water. Set aside.

Curry Sauce:

1. To prepare the Curry Sauce, heat the oil in a 6- to 8-quart nonstick saucepan. When hot, add garlic and sauté for about 20 seconds. Add onions and sauté over medium to high heat, stirring once every minute or so, until translucent, about 8 to 10 minutes. Add all the spices and salt, sauté for about 3 to 5 minutes and then add chopped tomatoes.

2. Stir and sauté for about 5 minutes, transfer to a food processor and grind the mixture for about 30 seconds in the food processor. Transfer back to the pot and place on low to medium heat; cover and slowly simmer for about 30 to 40 minutes, or until a sheen of oil is seen on the top. Check and stir every 5 minutes to make sure the sauce does not stick to the bottom of the pan. If that happens, reduce the heat slightly. The finished sauce should have the consistency of thick yogurt. If the sauce is thinner, remove the lid and boil off some of the liquid. If the sauce is too thick, add some water. Remove from heat and set aside.

Chicken:

1. In another 6- to 8-quart saucepan, heat 3 tablespoons oil. When very hot, add and sauté the chicken over high heat, stirring once every minute or so, for about 5 minutes. Add prepared curry sauce and cook over low heat, uncovered, for about 5 minutes. Set aside.

Toppings for Biriyani:

1. In a nonstick sauté pan, heat 5 tablespoons oil. When hot, add cashews and stir-fry till toasted and golden brown. Remove with a slotted spoon and set aside. In the same oil, fry raisins until they puff up. Remove with a slotted spoon and set aside. Add thinly sliced onions to the hot oil and sauté over high heat. Sauté onions until deep, crisp golden brown, stirring once every couple of minutes and adjusting the heat, as necessary. Set aside.

Rice:

1. In a 6- to 8-quart saucepot, heat 1 tablespoon oil. When hot, add black cumin seeds and sauté for about 10 to 15 seconds. Add rice and sir-fry for about 4 to 5 minutes. Add 2 cups of water. (This amount is less than water needed for fully cooking the rice. The rice will be partially cooked in the pot and finish cooking when the Biriyani is baked in the oven. If you have washed rice just before cooking, use only 1 1/2 cups of water). Add salt, cinnamon sticks and bay leaves, bring the water to a boil, reduce heat, cover and simmer about 10 to 12 minutes, or until all the water is absorbed. At this time, the rice is not fully cooked.

Putting it all together:

1. Assembly and baking of Biriyani: In a large, 8-quart casserole dish with a tight-fitting lid, arrange half of the rice in a layer at the bottom. Place the mixture of chicken and curry sauce over this rice in an even a layer, and then place remaining rice

over top of the chicken. Place the lid on the casserole and seal the lid all around with the dough. It would help if the dough were formed into thick spaghetti for this purpose. Seal the gap between the lid and the casserole by pressing the dough spaghetti in the gap. The dough seal will prevent steam from escaping and contents will be cooked by steam.

2. Place the casserole in an oven preheated to 300 degrees F. Bake for 1 hour; remove from the oven. When ready to eat, break and discard the dough seal. Sprinkle caramelized onions, nuts and raisins on top of the biriyani (photo on page 206).

Raita and Chutneys

Raitas and chutneys are side dishes served with meals in India. Raitas are yogurt-based dishes and make an excellent accompaniment, especially with spicy dishes, because of their cooling effect. This chapter includes a couple of my favorite raita recipes.

The word chutney has been made famous worldwide by "Major Grays Mango Chutney." In India, the word chutney is used generally for spicy dips served with appetizers. Some of the chutney recipes have been included in the feasts. Additional recipes are included in this chapter.

Kheeray Ka Raita

INGREDIENTS (Serves 4-6)

2 cups plain whole-milk yogurt

1/2 cucumber, seeded and cut into 1/4-inch dice

1/2 cup chopped cilantro

1 green chile pepper, chopped (optional)

1/2 teaspoon salt

1 teaspoon ground toasted cumin

1/2 teaspoon paprika or crushed chile peppers

1. In a 3 to 4 quart bowl, whisk yogurt for 2 minutes and then add and mix rest of the ingredients except cumin and paprika or crushed chile peppers. Sprinkle cumin and paprika or crushed chile peppers on top. Store in the refrigerator and serve cold. (See photo page 9.)

Kela Raita

1 tablespoon oil

2 teaspoon black mustard seeds

1 dry red chile pepper, cut in to pieces no larger than 1/4 inch

2 cups plain whole-milk yogurt

1 banana, peeled and cut into 1/4- to 1/2-inch dice

1/2 teaspoon salt

1/2 teaspoon paprika

1 teaspoon ground toasted cumin

1. Heat oil in a 4 quart saucepot. When hot, add mustard seeds and red chile pepper. The oil should be hot enough that mustard seeds pop. Turn the heat off as soon as mustard seeds stop popping, about 5 to 10 seconds. Mix in the remaining ingredients except cumin and stir well to incorporate. Transfer to a serving bowl and sprinkle cumin on top. Store in the refrigerator and serve cold.

Gajar Kai Chutney
(Indian Carrot Relish)

INGREDIENTS (Serves 8-10)

4 tablespoons oil

1 teaspoon black mustard seeds

1 teaspoons nigella seeds (optional)

6 to 8 cloves garlic, peeled and chopped fine

4 carrots, peeled and cut into 1-inch long, 1/2 inch thick sticks

1 teaspoon crushed chile peppers

1 teaspoon turmeric

2 teaspoons paprika

1 teaspoon salt

1/4 cup sugar

1/2 cup malt vinegar (if unavailable, substitute with white vinegar)

1. In a 6 quart saucepot, heat oil on high. When hot, add black mustard seeds and nigella seeds if using. Fry for about 10 seconds and then add chopped garlic. Fry for another 10 seconds and add the carrot sticks.

2. Sauté carrot sticks at high heat, stirring every minute or so, for about 3 to 4 minutes. Add crushed chile peppers, turmeric, paprika, and salt and stir-fry for about 2 minutes.

3 Add sugar and vinegar and cook on high, stirring as needed, until all the liquid is absorbed (about 3 to 5 minutes). Remove from stove and let cool. Serve at room temperature

4. Gajar Kai Chutney can be served as an accompaniment to the main meal. The relish can be stored in the refrigerator for up to 5 days. (See photo page 4.)

Yogurt-Cashew-Sour Cream Sauce

INGREDIENTS (Serves 6)

1/4 cup plain yogurt

1 cup ground cashews

1/4 cup sour cream

1 teaspoon sugar

1/2 teaspoon chile flakes

1/4 teaspoon salt

1. Thoroughly mix together all the ingredients. Yogurt-Cashew-Sour Cream Sauce makes a good garnish for Tandoori Asparagus. It can be stored for up to 4 days in the refrigerator.

Yogurt-Cashew-Tamarind Sauce

INGREDIENTS (Serves 6)

1/4 cup plain yogurt

1 cup ground cashews

1/4 cup Tamarind Concentrate (see page 26)

1 teaspoon sugar

1/2 teaspoon chile flakes

1/4 teaspoon salt

1. Thoroughly mix together all the ingredients. Yogurt-Cashew-Tamarind Sauce makes a good garnish for Tandoori Portobello Mushrooms. It can be stored for up to 4 days in the refrigerator.

Index